Immigration and the Public Sector in Denmark

Eskil Wadensjö and Helena Orrje

Immigration and the Public Sector in Denmark

AARHUS UNIVERSITY PRESS
THE ROCKWOOL FOUNDATION RESEARCH UNIT

Immigration and the public sector in Denmark
Copyright © The authors and Aarhus University Press 2002
Cover by Lotte Bruun Rasmussen
Printed in Denmark by the Narayana Press, Gylling

ISBN 87 7288 896 2

AARHUS UNIVERSITY PRESS

Langelandsgade 177
DK-8200 Aarhus N
Fax (+45) 89 42 53 80
www.unipress.dk

73 Lime Walk
Headington, Oxford OX3 7AD
Fax (+44) 1865 750 079

Box 511
Oakville, CT 06779
Fax (+1) 860 945 9468

Contents

Figures

Tables

Table 5.12. Total net transfers to the public sector (in million Danish *kroner*) for different groups in 1991, 1995, 1996, 1997 and 1998. (Amounts in 1997 prices in parentheses)

Table 6.1. Regression estimates (OLS) with net transfer to the public sector in 1998 (in thousand Danish *kroner*) as the dependent variable; and age, gender, family status, country of origin, employment rate and earnings as independent variables

Table 6.2. Regression estimates (OLS) with net transfer to the public sector in 1998 (in thousand Danish *kroner*) as the dependent variable; and age, gender, family status, country of origin, employment rate, hourly wages and earnings as independent variables for those who have a positive wage rate and who are not self-employed

Table 6.3. Regression estimates (OLS) with net transfer to the public sector (in thousand Danish *kroner* in 1997 prices) in 1996, 1997 and 1998 as the dependent variable; and age, gender, family status, country of origin and employment rate as independent variables

Table 6.4. Coefficient estimates of the effect of the rate of employment on net transfer to the public sector 1996, 1997 and 1998 for different groups

Table 6.A1. Regression estimates (OLS) with net transfer to the public sector in 1998 (in thousand Danish *kroner*) as dependent variable; and age, gender, family status, country of origin, length of stay in Denmark and employment rate as independent variables

Table 6.A2. Regression estimates (OLS) with net transfer to the public sector (in thousand Danish *kroner* in 1997 prices) in 1996, 1997 and 1998 as dependent variable; and age, gender, family status, country of origin, length of stay in Denmark and employment rate as independent variables

Table 7.1. Net transfers to the public sector (in Danish *kroner*) per person 18 years and older for different groups (with or without revision of net transfers to children) in the years 1991, 1995, 1996, 1997 and 1998. (Amounts in 1997 prices in parentheses)

Table 7.2. Net transfers to the public sector (in Danish *kroner*) per person 18 years and older from non-Western countries according to length of stay in Denmark (with or without revision of net transfers to children) in the years 1991, 1995, 1996, 1997 and 1998. (Amounts in 1997 prices in parentheses)

Table 7.3. Net transfers to the public sector (in Danish *kroner*) per person 18 years and older for different groups in 1998, excluding the net transfer to children according to two different methods, and 1995 according to the direct estimate method. (Amounts in 1998 prices in parentheses)

Foreword

In 1997 the Rockwool Foundation decided that 'immigrants and their living conditions' should be given a higher priority among the areas in which the Foundation seeks to present reliable and balanced social scientific knowledge to political decision-makers and to the public debate.

Some of the major questions to be answered by such research would include how the encounter between the new citizens and their descendents, on the one hand, and Danish society (including the labour market) on the other, takes place, and how it affects living conditions for immigrants and their descendents. An important factor in this connection is *how* integration into the Danish labour market takes place. From previous experience at the Rockwool Foundation Research Unit, and with the abundant data possibilities available in the official statistics, this area of research seemed to be a good place to concentrate initial efforts.

A pilot survey was carried out in the Research Unit in 1998-99 with the participation of several international experts in the field which, through analyses of the global demographic situation in general, and immigration to Denmark in particular, was designed to provide a broader background knowledge of the nature of immigration. The results were published in *Immigration to Denmark. International and national perspectives,* by David Coleman and Eskil Wadensjö (1999, Aarhus University Press).

Professor Eskil Wadensjö's contribution to the book consisted of an analysis of the general economic effects of immigration, with particular emphasis on redistribution via the public sector. The analyses were based on an extremely interesting data set, which the so-called Law Model from the then Ministry of Economics – now the Ministry of Finance – so kindly made available to Eskil Wadensjö. The first analysis was extended and elaborated in the next stage of the project stressing new empirical data for Denmark.

Eskil Wadensjö's results were published in their entirety in *Integration i Danmark omkring årtusindskiftet. Indvandrernes møde med arbejdsmarkedet og velfærdssamfundet* (*Integration in Denmark around the turn of the millennium. Immigrants' encounter with the labour market and the welfare society*) edited by Gunnar Viby Mogensen and Poul Chr. Matthiessen (2000, Aarhus University Press), and in more popular form in *Mislykket integration? (Abortive integration?)* by Gunnar Viby Mogensen and Poul Chr. Matthiessen (2000, Spektrum), with comments and assessments by Marianne Jelved, the then Minister of Economic Affairs.

As Eskil Wadensjö's data material and his analyses were of such a unique nature, we asked the Swedish researcher to continue researching within this field, and *Immigration and the Public Sector in Denmark* is the result of this work. We thank the Ministry of Finance for allowing us to use the data in the Law Model and for so kindly cooperating once again with Eskil Wadensjö and the Research Unit.

The project has of course been carried out by the Research Unit in complete scientific independence of both the Ministry and the Rockwool Foundation. That being said, however, it would have been difficult to carry out the project within such a generous financial framework without the helpful interest of the Foundation.

I owe the Foundation's staff, including its director Poul Erik Pedersen, and not least the Board and its chairman Tom Kähler, warm thanks for the usual high degree of co-operation between the Foundation and the Research Unit.

Copenhagen, June 2002

Gunnar Viby Mogensen

The Authors' Foreword

As mentioned by Gunnar Viby Mogensen, the Rockwool Foundation Research Unit's project on immigrants and their living conditions started in 1997. Earlier results from the part of this project that focused on the fiscal impact of immigration into Denmark have been published as chapters in three books from the project and in two articles published elsewhere.[1] The data presented in this publication covers a longer period than the project's earlier studies. It uses both panel data and cross-sectional data, it analyses the influences of earnings on the fiscal impact, and in many other respects this analysis is also an extension of the earlier studies.

We have enjoyed the support of many people in the preparation of this book. First of all we would like to thank the Rockwool Foundation Research Unit, and especially its leader Gunnar Viby Mogensen, for consistent and strong support of the study during its now more than three-year long history. We have received innumerable useful comments and ideas and have had many interesting discussions with Gunnar Viby Mogensen and members of the staff of the Rockwool Foundation Research Unit.

The data used in this study is from the Law Model previously localised in the Ministry of Economic Affairs, now in the Ministry of Finance. We wish to express gratitude to the Ministry for its very positive attitude to independent research based on their data. We especially thank Frederik Hansen for assistance with the data and for answering our many questions. We have learnt a great deal from him, not only about the data of the Law Model, but also about the Danish economy and the rules and structure of the public sector in Denmark.

Some sections of this book, or its entire contents, have been presented at various conferences and seminars: the EALE conference in Jyväskylä; a conference organized by the Swedish Ministry of International Affairs in Stockholm; seminars held at the Aarhus School of Business, at the Department of Economics at the University of Gothenburg, the Rockwool Foundation Research Unit, and the Swedish Institute for Social Research at Stockholm University. Thanks go to the participants and especially to those who were commentators.

---

1   See Wadensjö (1999), (1999a), (2000), (2000a) and Gunnar Viby Mogensen and Poul Chr. Matthiessen (2000).

We also want to thank Søren Brodersen, Jan Ekberg, Björn Gustafsson, Frederik Hansen, Ronald Lee, Timothy Miller and David Wildasin for their comments on the entire manuscript or parts of it.

We wish also to sincerely thank Jean Parr and Mary Waters Lund for their help in reviewing our English.

Stockholm, June 2002

Eskil Wadensjö and Helena Orrje

Chapter 1

Economic Effects of Immigration:
The Background

Immigration has effects for the migrants as well as the countries of origin and destination. The focus of this study is on the effects of immigration on the public sector in Denmark. Denmark has been a net immigration country since the 1960s, but the number entering the country has grown considerably in the last decade. In this chapter some background information is presented on immigration into Denmark and on the immigrants living there. The fiscal impact dealt with in this book is only one of the effects of immigration on the Danish economy. To set the study of the fiscal impact in perspective, some of the other effects are discussed in this chapter. In the concluding section of the chapter, an outline of the book is presented.

1.1 Denmark – an immigration country[2]

As in other Scandinavian countries, emigration from Denmark was high in the 19th and early part of the 20th centuries. Many left Denmark for North America and other countries outside Europe. At the same time, immigrants arrived from neighbouring countries like Sweden and from the area which today constitutes the southern part of Poland, but all in all Denmark had a net emigration. In the first decades following World War II quite a few people left Denmark and moved to Sweden, which at that time had higher wages and lower unemployment.

In the late 1960s unemployment became very low in Denmark and problems with recruiting workers increased. Some employers started to recruit outside of Denmark, whilst many people also came on their own initiative to look for jobs. This immigration consisted mainly of blue-collar workers, who generally ended up in jobs for the unskilled. Compared to other West-European countries such as France, Germany, the Netherlands, Sweden, Switzerland and the U.K., Denmark became a country of immigration relatively late. However, Denmark's period of 'importing' labour was short. In connection with the first oil crisis in 1973, the unemployment rate rose sharply and became even higher from the end of the decade.

---

2 See Coleman & Wadensjö (1999), Ejby Poulsen & Lange (1998) and Schultz-Nielsen et al. (2001) for more detailed information on immigration to Denmark and the immigrant population.

The unemployment crisis of the 1970s put a stop to labour immigration of the kind typical in the late 1960s. But it did not stop other types of immigration. The number of refugees entering Denmark increased in the 1970s and especially during the 1980s and the 1990s. The net immigration rose greatly as the inflow was higher and the refugees for obvious reasons had a lower propensity to return to their home countries than the earlier labour migrants. Another large group of new immigrants consists of relatives to earlier immigrants – both labour immigrants and refugees. Part of this flow of relatives can be explained by the fact that it is common among some groups of immigrants to find a suitable wife or husband in their home country. The labour immigrants of the 1960s and the refugees of the 1980s and 1990s have come mainly from countries outside Europe or from countries in Europe that have a lower economic standard.

Besides the labour force and refugee immigration described above, there has always been migration between Denmark and other industrialised countries. Mobility has been facilitated in that Denmark has belonged to the common Nordic labour market since the 1950s and to the common EU labour market since the 1970s. Immigration from Western countries has tended to increase during the last decade but is less than migration from non-Western countries. Many of these immigrants return to their home countries after a few years in Denmark. In the same way, many Danes move to other Western countries for shorter or longer periods of time.

It is mainly skilled or professional people who migrate from Western countries. More often than not they go directly into jobs that, in many cases, are high positions. This means that the Western and non-Western migration flows are to a large extent phenomena of different types and also that the effects differ in many respects.

TABLE 1.1.
Migration to and from Denmark 1931-2000. Yearly average for each decade

DECADE	IMMIGRATION (YEARLY AVERAGE)	EMIGRATION (YEARLY AVERAGE)
1931/1940	12,000	9,800
1941/1950	14,041	15,755
1951/1960	21,358	25,594
1961/1970	30,146	27,420
1971/1980	33,488	30,879
1981/1990	33,845	29,574
1991/2000	49,756	36,649

Source: Statistics Denmark, *Statistisk Årbog 2001*, Copenhagen.

TABLE 1.2.

Immigrants living in Denmark in 1980, 1990 and 2000. First and second generations

COUNTRY OF ORIGIN	FIRST-GENERATION IMMIGRANTS			SECOND-GENERATION IMMIGRANTS		
	1980	1990	2000	1980	1990	2000
Europe	104,676	114,826	170,057	12,910	20,825	40,052
Africa	4,846	8,725	26,837	775	2,111	9,058
North America	6,408	6,099	7,064	1,053	918	983
South and Central America	2,831	3,990	5,945	247	340	564
Asia	15,204	46,085	84,458	3,109	9,107	30,201
Oceania	559	672	1,261	106	84	123
Total	134,705	181,109	296,924	18,253	33,462	81,241

Note: The difference between the total and the sum of the groups in the table consists of people for whom information on origin is missing.

Source: Statistics Denmark, *Statistisk Årbog 2001*, Copenhagen.

The long-range development of migration to and from Denmark is shown in Table 1.1. Note that the numbers include migration of both foreign and Danish citizens. For example, 22,105 of the 52,915 people who immigrated into Denmark in the year 2000 were Danish citizens (Danes returning from a stay outside Denmark). Of the 43,417 people who emigrated from Denmark that year, 26,887 were Danish citizens.[3] The large and increasing immigration of non-Danish citizens has led to an increase in the number of immigrants living in Denmark and also of second generation immigrants. In Table 1.2 the number of first-generation immigrants[4] living in Denmark in 1980, 1990 and 2000 as well as the corresponding development in the number of second-generation immigrants[5] are shown.

---

3   Among those of active age, there is a net emigration of Danish citizens and a net immigration of non-Danish citizens. A comparison of different groups of non-Danish citizens as regards immigration and emigration shows that in 1999 the number of immigrants from OECD countries other than Denmark exceeded the number of emigrants from the same countries by 50 per cent. For citizens from other European countries and from other parts of the world the number of immigrants was several times larger than the number of emigrants. See Dansk Arbejdsgiverforening (2001), p. 46.

4   First-generation immigrants are defined as those who were born outside Denmark and whose parents were born outside Denmark or (at the time of immigration) were foreign citizens.

5   Second-generation immigrants are defined as those who were born in Denmark, and none of their parents were born in Denmark.

As seen from Table 1.2 the number of immigrants has increased considerably during the last two decades, especially the number of immigrants from Asia and Africa. Among European immigrants, the groups who were born in Turkey and the former Yugoslavia have the largest growth.[6]

The growth in the number of second-generation immigrants is even larger with the Asian and African groups growing the fastest. The majority of immigrants upon arrival in Denmark are young adults. So this fact, combined with a higher fertility rate among non-Western immigrants, means that the size of the second-generation population is relatively large and fast growing.[7]

1.2 Different economic effects of immigration

International migration can result from economic and other circumstances. Refugees account for a large amount of the international migration seen in recent decades, and they have come to form a large group in Denmark. Family members joining relatives who have already migrated comprise an even larger group of immigrants in Denmark. Whatever the cause of migration, the phenomenon produces economic effects in the host country and elsewhere. Immigration can influence the economy of the host country in several ways, both directly and indirectly. Directly, immigration can influence wages and prices. Among the indirect effects of immigration are those which influence the public sector and economic policy. These indirect effects can be divided into two groups. The first group results from the fact that the public sector redistributes resources among individuals and groups of individuals on the basis of factors such as family status, age and labour market circumstances. The immigration of a group involves a transfer from and to the group, via taxes, transfers and public consumption. This can result in net transfers to and from the rest of the population. The second group of factors that affect public policy result from the fact that immigration can influence a country's economy and, thereby, also indirectly influence the circumstances on which economic policy is based, as well as that policy itself. Finally, there are other kinds of indirect effects, which are not related to the public sector and policy.

The effects of immigration can be divided into four categories: 1) effects on wages and prices, 2) effects on public sector redistribution, 3) macro-effects (effects on un-

---

6   See Statistics Denmark (2001), p. 193.
7   See Stephensen (2001) for information on the present fertility rates of different groups and prediction for their future development. The fertility rate of Western immigrants is lower than that of the Danish population.

employment and inflation and thus also on the basis upon which economic policy is formed), and 4) various kinds of indirect effects. This chapter reviews international studies on the various areas and attempts to relate the findings of this literature to immigration into Denmark.

Immigration not only influences the economy of the host country, but also the economic situation of individual immigrants and the economies of the countries of origin. An immigrant's own situation can be transformed as a result of migrating to a new country. Immigration of foreigners in search of work is precisely this kind of migration; from unemployment or risk of unemployment and low wages to employment and higher wages. This does not mean that all who emigrate in order to secure a better job actually end up earning higher wages; it merely means that an expectation of higher earnings is a motivating factor in the migration. In the case of refugees, considerations other than economic factors lie behind the decision to migrate. Even in such cases, however, a higher economic standard can result from the migration, and the economic situation in potential host countries, including the system of support from the public sector, can be a factor in the choice of the country to which the refugee will migrate. Countries from which people emigrate can, in the same way as the new country, be influenced economically via direct and indirect effects. Wages and prices can be influenced, and emigration can have fiscal and economic effects that influence the economic policy. Economic effects on immigrants themselves and on the countries from which they migrate will not be treated in this chapter, although a more thorough evaluation of the economic effects of international migration would have to take these factors into account.

1.3 Effects on wages

Let us begin by discussing – with the help of a traditional economic model – the effects of immigration on wages and prices, while temporarily ignoring the existence of a public sector that is involved in various resource-redistribution schemes. A country's output depends on the level of factors of production (labour and capital), on the relationship between the factors of production and production itself (which, in turn, is dependent upon the country's level of technological and organisational advancement), and on the degree to which the production factors are utilised (unemployment and unutilised production capacity are signs that the production factors are not being fully utilised). Immigration increases the size of the labour force in the host country. The balance between the production factors is altered if immigration is not accompanied by an equivalent influx of capital. The number of workers per unit of capital increases. This, in turn, has consequences for wages, returns on capital, and also for the cost of goods and services. Equally important are potential

changes in the structure of the labour force. Labour is not a homogeneous production factor but can, for example, be divided according to region, industry, occupation and education.

Immigration, then, means that the size of the labour force in the host country increases. This, in turn, leads to a fall in wages and a rise in returns on capital. Wage
levels will fall provided that three basic conditions are met: 1) that the immigration
is not accompanied by a parallel influx of capital to ensure that the capital intensity
of the country is maintained; 2) that wages equal the value of the marginal product
of labour; and 3) the absence of economies of scale in the economy.

Let us briefly examine these three conditions.

The first condition is that immigration is not accompanied by an influx of capital
that is large enough to allow the capital intensity to be maintained. It is not self-
evident that this condition is always met. Historically, for example, emigration to
North America was accompanied by a parallel injection of capital into North America, even if the capital did not always originate in the same country as the immigrants.[8]
Today's international migration also provides examples of a close relationship
between the mobility of the labour force and that of capital. This is especially true of
the "new Asian emigration" from countries such as Hong Kong, Taiwan, Singapore
and South Korea. This particular migratory trend is partly based on the fact that
some countries grant immigration visas to immigrants who also invest in the economy of the host country.[9] Even setting aside this type of very close connection
between the movement of labour and capital, the argument can be made that capital
is so mobile today that movements of labour, and the accompanying altered wage
relations, lead to movements of capital in the same direction. However, no empirical
research into the existence or extent of this relationship between the movement of
labour and capital in the 1990s has yet been conducted.

That wages match the value of the marginal contribution of labour is a standard
assumption in economics that is also open to question. The Scandinavian economies display a considerable rigidity in wage formation, so that an increase in the
number of workers does not directly lead to lower wages. Powerful trade unions and

---

8   Brinley Thomas has examined this particular issue most thoroughly. See, for example, Thom-
    as (1972).
9   See Tseng (1997) for a review of the problem and an investigation of this type of migration
    from Taiwan.
10 Trade unions aware of the fact that it is the number of available jobs more than wage levels that
    influence immigration may, at an enlargement of the common labour market, be inclined to
    keep wages high to reduce the incentives for people from other countries to move to the coun-
    try. See Lundborg (1997).

implicit or explicit wage contracts generally prevent, in any case, nominal wages from falling when the number of workers rises.[10] Still, the effect can be that wages rise less quickly than they would have had the size of the labour force not increased due to immigration, and thus that wages do adjust, but over a longer period of time. One might also argue that wages paid to immigrants are lower than the market rate (i.e. their wages are lower than the value of their contribution) because of, for example, discrimination. In this case, the economic gain reaped by the country's native population is larger.[11]

As regards the third condition, that there are no economies of scale in the country's production, it is hardly probable that any clear economies of scale will be available in countries that form a customs union. A company's 'domestic' market in such cases will include not only the market in the home country but also that in all the countries of the union. On the other hand, economies of scale can be seen in certain types of public consumption. We will return to this matter later.

Immigration means that economic production capacity rises. Since remuneration falls when the size of the labour force grows, the wages earned by immigrants do not entirely match the increase in production that immigration creates, given that wages are equal to the value of the marginal contribution.[12] This means that the existing population in the host country will reap an economic gain from immigration. While it is true that the native labour force will see a decrease in wages, this decrease will be more than compensated by an increase in returns on capital. The way in which this affects individual members of the society depends on how capital is distributed. If one imagines that capital is distributed equally among the entire native labour force, then the result would be that everyone wins. A more realistic picture is that capital is distributed in such a way that some segments of the labour force win while others lose.

To what extent does immigration affect wages? This depends on how wage-sensitive the demand for labour is. Wage-sensitivity can be measured by the degree of elasticity in the demand for labour. The estimates of the elasticity of labour demand vary widely, but a fairly reasonable estimation is that it is about 0.3.[13] As immigration in any one year constitutes only a small part of the population, the wage effect is small compared to the average yearly wage change. The effect is even smaller if immigrant participation in the labour force is low.

---

11 See Dex (1992) for an early review of research on discrimination against immigrants. There are several studies indicating that discrimination of immigrants may exist in different countries. See Golder (2000) for Switzerland.

12 This is the standard result. See, however, Lundborg & Segerstrom (1998) for an analysis of a model (with endogenous economic growth) where the result is a fall in the return on capital.

13 See Hamermesh (1993) for a general survey of research on labour demand.

Probably more important than the fact that immigration influences the capital intensity is the fact that it also influences the composition of the labour force. This influence is important, as research on the demand for labour shows that a simplified analysis using only a single type of labour fails to reveal significant relations. One result is that different types of labour are not, in many cases, substitutes, but complements in the production process. If a certain part of the labour force grows because of immigration, and wages then fall for this group, it may also imply an increase in demand and higher wages for other groups that complement the first group in the production process.[14]

We have long been aware that the way in which immigrants divide into various industries and occupations has an impact on wages, and this knowledge has influenced immigration policy in various countries. Ashley Timmer and Jeffrey Williamson (1998) have produced an interesting historical study of immigration policy in Argentina, Australia, Brazil, Canada and the United States during the period 1860-1930. Their hypothesis – which they are also able to support – is that immigration policy during this period was formed so as to preserve the relative wage differentials between skilled and unskilled workers. We can also study the debate about immigration that took place in the 1960s in countries such as Denmark and Sweden. Resistance to immigration in both countries was strongest among groups whose wages were most likely to be influenced by job-related immigration, i.e. primarily among unskilled workers.[15]

One way in which we might analyse a case of two different groups on the labour market might be to work with a model with two production factors, namely two different types of workers: skilled workers and unskilled workers. Immigrants are presumed to belong to the second group (or presumed not to be able to use their education in the country of destination). We can then produce an analysis, which is consistent with that in the previous section, where the production factors were labour and capital. The result is that skilled workers see an increase in wages, while unskilled see lower wages because of immigration.

One problem with this analysis is that it does not allow for the possibility that these groups can be complements to each other, as well as substitutes. It thus makes more sense to employ a model with (at least) three production factors: capital, skilled workers, and unskilled workers. Estimates indicate that the two categories of workers complement each other in production (while capital and unskilled workers are substitutes).

---

14   See for example Bauer (1998) for a study of the effects in Germany.
15   For Denmark, see Jensen (2001).

An examination of how immigrants are distributed in industries and occupations suggests that immigrants are over-represented in low-wage jobs that only require a brief period of training,[16] but also in certain professions that require a lengthy education (under-representation is especially pronounced in jobs that fall between these categories).[17] Immigrants are under-represented above all in jobs that require highly advanced skills in the language, culture or formal and informal rules of the host country. This is the case, for example, with many white-collar occupations. In Denmark, as in other Nordic countries, immigrants from countries with more highly developed economies are over-represented among the highest-paid workers, while immigrants from countries with less developed economies are over-represented among the lowest-paid workers.[18]

In general, immigrants are also highly over-represented in certain regions. In most countries, immigrants are primarily over-represented in large cities. In Denmark, an average of 7.1 per cent of the population consists of immigrants and their children in 2000.[19] In the Danish capital, Copenhagen, and surrounding areas, this percentage is significantly higher (13.9) and in some municipalities within this area – for instance in the Municipality of Copenhagen (17.6), and suburbs such as Ishøj (24.2), Brøndby (21.1) and Albertslund (20.0) – it is even higher. Outside the Copenhagen region, the percentage is especially high in larger cities such as Aarhus and Odense, and in some of the municipalities along the border to Germany. The percentages are much higher in some areas of these municipalities.[20]

The effects on wages can be greater for some occupations, educational groups and regions than for the labour force as a whole, due to the selectivity of immigration. The wage effect depends, among other things, on the degree of geographic and job-related mobility among the native labour force. Increased movement away from regional labour markets with a high density of immigrants and decreased settlement in such markets can thus reduce the effect on wages.[21] The mobility among the immigrants and the selectivity as regards region, occupation and education among those of the immigrants leaving the country can also influence the wage effect.

---

16   Bauer et al. (1999) indicate in a study of the German labour market that the foreign workers are strongly over-represented in workplaces that have a high risk for severe accidents.

17   For the US labour market, see for example Trejo (1999).

18   See Ejby Poulsen & Lange (1998) and Emerek, Jacobsen & Dahl (1998).

19   Figures taken from Statistics Denmark, Statistikbanken.

20   See Hummelgaard et al. (1995) for a discussion of the concentration of immigrants within certain residential areas.

21   Card & DiNardo (2001) do not find a selective outmigration of natives as a response to immigration in local labour markets in the U.S.

There are two basic types of studies of the effects of immigration on wages.[22] The first type is based on differences between the percentage of immigrants living in various regions or in different occupations. This type of study generally shows only a minimal effect on wages.[23] One explanation of why the expected effects do not appear might be that a movement of immigrants to an area is entirely or partly countered by changes of the settlement patterns of the native population, and by a movement of capital to the area to which the immigrants have moved. The other type of study is based on a view of the country as a single economic entity. The study of this entity is then based on the fact that variations in the composition of production factors can be traced over time. In this type of study, immigration appears to have a considerably greater effect on wages.

An interesting question is whether immigrants comprise a non-competitive group, by occupying a segment of the labour market and holding jobs that the native population does not want and, thereby, widening the range of goods and services on the market. Daniel Hamermesh's (1997) study of the American labour market fails to find any evidence to support this hypothesis. The group that, to a certain extent, holds these kinds of jobs consists of non-immigrants, namely African-Americans. It should, however, be noted that Hamermesh's analysis does not take into account illegal immigrants, who are perhaps more likely to hold such jobs (but for whom statistics are lacking), nor does it include the self-employed. We will return to self-employed immigrants later.

For several decades following the end of World War II, wages and incomes underwent a process of levelling out in industrialised countries. During the past two decades, however, this trend has been reversed, and differences have been increasing. In analyses of this development, attention has mainly been drawn to the question of labour demand, but also to some extent to that of labour supply.

---

22   See Borjas, Freeman & Katz (1996) for a discussion of both types of studies.

23   A recently published study of the United States, Enchautegui (1997), indicates, however, that immigration accounts for only a small part of the decrease in wages for high school dropouts nationally, but that it has a larger effect on areas where large numbers of immigrants live.

24   Globalisation is not a new phenomenon. On the contrary, increasing globalisation is a distinguishing feature of the 19th and early 20th centuries, until the outbreak of World War I. International migration played a considerably greater role during this period of globalisation than in the present period. Following an initial period marked by increasing differences in wages between countries, most of the period before World War I saw decreasing differences in wages. See Williamson (1998). It should be noted that there are large differences between the economies of the 19th century and those of the 21st century. The public sector for example has a much more important role in the present-day economies than in those of the heyday of international migration in the 19th century.

As to the question of labour demand, three explanatory factors have figured prominently in the debate: an increasing internationalisation of economies (globalisation),[24] technological advances and changes in the organization of work places.

The deregulation of international trade (lower tariffs, fewer and less restrictive non-tariff barriers) and lower transport costs have led to greater international competition and thus increased specialisation. Industrial countries with more highly developed economies ('the North') have come to specialise in making products that require a relatively large, highly educated labour force (which is relatively plentiful in these countries), while countries with less developed economies ('the South') have specialised in making products that require a relatively large labour force without such education (which is relatively plentiful in these countries). This has resulted, relatively speaking, in an increased demand for more highly educated workers in more highly developed countries such as Denmark.

Technological development does not take any particular direction through physical necessity. It can tend towards the use of relatively larger numbers of workers with less formal education or towards the use of larger numbers of highly educated workers. In recent decades, the trend in technological development seems to have been to make do with fewer less educated workers. Therefore, the demand for this type of worker has been falling. Employers are seeking more highly educated workers and this development influences demand in both the more and the less developed countries.

The third factor that influences changes in labour demand is related to the way in which labour is organised at the workplace. The development has gone from a more hierarchical form of labour organisation with clearly defined tasks for different jobs to a less hierarchical form of organisation where employees carry out more loosely defined tasks and are assumed to change tasks more frequently. This demands greater social and communicative skills from employees, which in turn leads to an increased need for a more highly educated labour force. Such changes, which would also include the requirement for greater skills in the language of the host country, could also lead to a decrease in the demand for immigrant workers.[25]

Denmark and other highly developed countries, have a steadily increasing demand for highly educated workers. In isolation, this could be expected to lead to greater wage differentials between more highly educated workers and those with less education. This, however, is counteracted by the fact that due to an increase in the educational level of young people, the labour supply has come to consist of a large number of well-educated people. In many countries, though, this expansion in edu-

---

25   See Broomé, Bäcklund, Lundh & Ohlsson (1996).

cation does not appear to have been comprehensive enough or to have taken place quickly enough to be able to neutralise the change in labour demand. This change in the composition of the labour force towards a greater proportion of more highly educated workers can also have been countered in some countries by the fact that many immigrants are less educated than the host country's population (or have an education that cannot be used on the labour market in the host country).

It has been suggested that the development in the United States has led primarily to an increase in wage differences, while the development in Europe has led mainly to an increase in unemployment differences. The cause of such differences between these two parts of the world might be that wages are more flexible in the United States than in Europe, due to weaker trade unions in the United States. In both cases, however, the result has been greater income differences. Immigration can, if immigrants with higher education are under-represented, contribute to an increased wage differential, and by leading to an increase in returns on capital, lead to further differences in income. Especially in the United States, the role that immigrants may play as a factor in growing wage differences has been the subject of lively debate.

If returns on education rise, then differences between the average wage earned by the native population and that earned by immigrants will also increase, given the difference in educational level between the two groups. In the case of the United States, increased returns on education have been very important in explaining growing differences between the average wage earned by the native population and that earned by immigrants.[26]

1.4 Effects on prices

Via effects on the wage structure, immigration can influence prices, for example by increasing the supply of labour in certain sectors that produce for the domestic market, thereby putting pressure on the prices of the goods and services they produce. If the immigrants' structure of demand differs from that of the non-immigrant population this can also influence the relative prices. Immigration can also lead to the establishment of markets for goods or services that were not previously available. In many countries, immigrants will typically establish themselves as entrepreneurs in certain sectors of the economy. One reason for this can be that they find it difficult to enter the normal labour market. They are not able to secure employment by offering to work for low wages – minimum wages, trade union agreements or social conventions about what constitutes reasonable remuneration for work

---

26   See Butcher & DiNardo (1998) for an empirical investigation of the development in the USA.

prevent their doing so. An alternative for them is then to start their own businesses. Restrictions on what constitutes a minimum hourly wage do not apply to people who are self-employed. Many small business owners work a great many hours for a very low hourly wage. In many cases, other family members also work in businesses owned by immigrants. Another reason why many immigrants start their own businesses is that some immigrant groups uphold traditions and have knowledge from their home country about how such businesses should be run, and perhaps also the fact that starting a business can make them more independent.[27]

Businesses run by immigrants are often concentrated in particular sectors, such as restaurants, retail shops and household services. A common feature for all of these businesses is that they do not require a great deal of capital to be established. In a comparison of all those in employment in Denmark, the proportion of immigrants from less developed countries who run their own businesses is higher.[28] The figures are 16 per cent for immigrants from less highly developed countries, 10 per cent for immigrants from more highly developed countries and 8 per cent for Danes.[29] The pattern for those sectors in which the self-employed work varies greatly from group to group, especially between immigrants from countries with less developed economies and Danes. Among immigrants from these countries, the majority – 71 per cent – are in the retail trade or the hotel/restaurant business, while self-employed Danes are distributed more evenly across the sectors, with the largest number (28 per cent) in farming.

The establishment of businesses run by immigrants can also give rise to effects on income distribution. The appearance of these effects depends in part on who the customers of such businesses are, and in part on the kinds of businesses with which immigrant-run businesses compete.

Which groups buy most goods and services from businesses run by immigrants? Some immigrant businesses are set up to serve the needs of the immigrants themselves. In many countries, there is a tendency for immigrant enclaves to develop, where many of the businesses are run by the immigrants themselves. Yet businesses run by immigrants do not necessarily cater to other immigrants alone. In many cases, the immigrant business will serve as a low-cost alternative, selling goods and

---

27   See Schultz-Nielsen et al. (2001) for Denmark.

28   If we examine the entire population within the respective groups, the proportion of self-employed is approximately the same, 4 per cent. The discrepancy between this figure and those in the text is due to the fact that a much lower percentage of immigrants from countries with less highly developed economies are employed, and so the self-employed constitute a larger portion of the total number of employed in the group.

29   See Ejby Poulsen & Lange (1998).

certain types of services, and will perhaps therefore cater primarily to low-income groups such as students.

The establishment of businesses that pay low hourly wages to the owner and family members can threaten the existence of other businesses whose owners view the issue of remuneration for labour differently.[30] Yet in many cases, immigrant businesses establish themselves in areas where there is no competition and where they almost seem to be competing with and replacing work normally carried out in the household, for example, eating out rather than at home or sending out sewing to a tailor.

Immigrants may also influence prices by their demand for goods and services. One example is the housing market. The housing prices may increase especially if the immigrants are concentrated to some parts of the market and if the supply side of the market is responding slowly to the increase in demand. Such a change in the demand for housing may also have redistributive effects and especially those who demand housing in the same segment of the market may lose.

1.5 Macro-economic effects

Immigration can influence unemployment. The exact nature of this influence, however, is not clear. It depends upon the way in which the structure of labour demand and labour supply are influenced by the immigration. One case that has been dealt with in various studies is the way in which immigration influences the state of the economy, or more generally whether immigration helps to exaggerate swings in the economy, or contributes to promoting stability. How do investments (private, public), consumption (private, public) and production look in the period immediately following a wave of immigration? Immigration can lead, for example, to investment in jobs (companies see a chance to expand), residential property and infrastructure, so that the total level of demand rises.

Does a larger wave of immigration and an increase in the immigrant population lead to greater unemployment? A superficial investigation does not support this hypothesis. It seems as if unemployment levels are determined by other factors, for example by a political desire to keep inflation at bay. Lower unemployment levels lead to higher inflation. In a way, one could say that the contribution that unemployment makes to the economy is to fight inflation, and that the unemployed are, in part, compensated for their efforts and, in part, contribute themselves to the control

---

30 A study by Farlie & Meyer (1997) deals with the question of whether immigrant businesses (especially those owned by Asian immigrants) threaten the existence of businesses owned by African-Americans. They do not find any evidence to support this hypothesis.

of inflation by having a lower standard of living.[31] The question is whether an unemployed immigrant contributes as much to holding inflation down as an unemployed Dane. (Actually, this is a matter that it should be possible to research, by including unemployment among Danes and unemployment among immigrants separately in the wage equations). If the immigrant does contribute as much, one could say that the Danish population has managed to attain a certain given (low) inflation level along with lower unemployment for themselves by allowing the immigrants to 'take over' a part of the unemployment that is needed to fight inflation.

It might also be the case that immigration leads to an increase in structural unemployment. Immigration leads to an increase in the labour supply in certain occupations and not so much in other types. This can, at least in the short term, lead to imbalances in the labour market if no adjustment of relative wages occurs, or via mobility between different occupations. Without an adjustment, the total level of unemployment may increase at any given level of inflation.

1.6 Outline of the book

In Chapter 2 the general principles for calculating the fiscal impact of immigration are presented. Some of the choices to be made in the analysis and different alternative formulations of the research problem are shown. In Chapter 3 the results from studies of the effects of immigration on the public sector finances in various countries are covered. Chapter 4 presents the database, the Law Model, utilized for the present study. This database is based on a sample of 3 per cent of the population living in Denmark.

Chapters 5-9 constitute the main part of the book. They contain different analyses of the fiscal impact of immigration to Denmark. In Chapter 5 the aggregate effects in the 1990s are studied and are related to the demographic structure and the labour market situation for immigrants. In Chapter 6-9 the analysis is based on individual observations. In Chapter 6 the factors that influence the individual net transfer to the public sector in cross-section data is studied. In Chapter 7 the net transfer over the life cycle is in focus. In that chapter the total net transfer effect of immigration in a specific year is also calculated. In Chapter 8 the analysis is based on a panel with information from 1995 and 1998. The panel data makes it possible to study the stability of the pattern on the individual level over time and also to corroborate the results from the cross-section studies. The theme of Chapter 9 centers around the effects on different parts of the public sector. Chapter 10 contains a summary and conclusions.

---

31 For an analysis in this line of thought that relies on the efficiency wages theory, see Epstein & Hillman (2000).

Chapter 2
Calculating the Fiscal Impact
of Immigration: Principles[32]

In the preceding chapter, the effects of immigration, aside from those for the public sector, were discussed. In this chapter and in the rest of the book, we will focus on the process of redistribution that is carried out via the public sector. The underlying question is: What are the effects of an inflow of immigrants on the population already residing in the country in terms of the revenues and expenditures of the public sector? The basic idea is that if revenues rise more than expenditure, then resources will be redistributed in favour of the existing population, while the opposite will result if expenditure rises more than revenues. The question we pose is whether the fiscal impact is positive or negative.

This chapter will deal with more basic issues, in order to provide the background for an examination in the following chapters of the results of the study of this problem in Denmark. These more basic issues will be covered in a few simple steps. We begin by discussing the structure of the entire system of redistribution, in order to then examine the various types of public sector activities. We will examine revenues (i.e. tax revenues), as well as the different costs related to public transfer payments and public consumption and investment. We will then proceed to examine the demarcation of the population in order to discuss some alternative analytical principles. In the next chapter we will present the results of some previous studies for different countries.

Individuals are consumers throughout their entire lives, but are only active in production for part of this time. Children are not allowed to take employment, and the age at which individuals enter the labour force has gradually been rising. After a period of employment, individuals typically enjoy a number of years as pensioners. What they produce during their 'active' lives must not only meet the needs of their own consumption in that period, but also cover consumption expenses for people of a 'passive' age, i.e. children and the elderly. This is made possible by means of a process of redistribution between the generations. This process takes place in mainly three different ways: via the family (for example, parents who provide for their chil-

---

32 For surveys of the principles for calculating the fiscal impacts of immigration see Lee (2001) and Lee & Miller (1997).

dren), via the market (for example, working individuals who invest in a pension in-surance) or via the public sector (two examples would be publicly financed schools and a pension system funded by tax revenues).[33] Redistribution via the public sector has come to be ever more important.

The redistribution of resources is carried out not only between generations, but also between individuals of an 'active' age. An important form of this type of redis-tribution is that which takes place between those who are employed and those who are not employed or who hold a job but cannot work, for example, due to illness. Re-sources are also redistributed from people earning high wages or having high in-comes to those earning low wages and with low incomes. This is done in part via a tax system in which the amount of tax paid increases along with an increase in in-come (even more so if the tax system is progressive), and in part via the transfer system. On the other hand, individual-oriented public consumption is generally not dependent upon the individual's wage or income, but mainly on other attributes like age, and other types of public consumption and investment are mainly related to the size of the population.

Immigration can influence redistribution via the public sector in different ways. In most societies, immigrants are over-represented among those of an active age. This should imply that resources are transferred from them to the rest of society, provided that all factors other than age are equal for both groups. On the other hand, in Denmark and most other European countries employment levels are lower among non-Western immigrants, and their average wage level is lower, all of which would suggest a transfer to the immigrants. The matter of the direction in which re-sources are actually transferred is an empirical question, and the answer varies from country to country and within a given country over a period of time.

It should also be noted that redistribution via the public sector may influence the size and structure of international migration just as local public taxes and expend-itures may influence internal migration.[34]

2.1 Different forms of public revenues and expenditures

The public sector obtains revenues from taxes and fees and has expenditures for transfer payments and for public consumption and investment. Both revenues and expenditures are influenced by immigration. We will treat the different parts in turn.

---

33   To this could be added redistribution by private relief organizations.
34   See for example Wildasin (1992, 1998 and 2000).

Immigrants contribute to public sector finances by paying taxes and various special fees, such as those paid for unemployment insurance and pensions. One problem in relating taxes to individuals and groups is that it is not always clear who actually pays the taxes. It is easy to determine who pays some taxes. Income tax, for
example, can be attributed to the person who formally pays the tax. A fairly easy
solution can also be found for some other taxes. Value-added tax and selective
purchase tax can be allocated in proportion to the consumption level of different individuals and households, and general payroll taxes can be distributed in proportion
to wages. The most difficult taxes to distribute are business taxes (taxes on profits,
environment taxes, etc.). The degree of uncertainty surrounding this point, as well as
many others, means that the type of calculations in which we are engaged should be
interpreted cautiously.

Transfers intended for specific individuals are easy to distribute. They are simply
traced to the individual in question. It is more difficult, however, to find an appropriate principle for the granting of subsidies to businesses (in many cases it might
not be appropriate to distribute them on individuals). Each of these transfers must
be examined separately to see what the relevant principle of distribution is.

It is possible to find a simplified method for the analysis of the social insurance
systems. This is primarily the case for systems in which compensation is actuarially
correct, i.e. where the insurance is run according to the same principles as a private
insurance. This can be the case for certain pension systems. If so, both disburse-
ments and receipts can be eliminated from the calculations. There are also other
cases in which the element of redistribution within national insurance can be distin-
guished from the element that is calculated in an actuarially correct manner, and
where only the subsidy element (with a negative or positive sum for a given individual) can be included in the calculations. One step in this direction is to carry out
a thorough analysis of various national insurance systems in order to see which
elements relate to insurance and which elements constitute redistribution in the
system.[35]

Public sector consumption can be divided into several different parts: 1) a part
which is independent of the size of the population, 2) a part where the extent of public sector activity depends upon the size and composition of the population, but
where it is not possible to tie a particular unit to a particular person, and 3) a part

---

35 See Gustman & Steinmeier (1998) for an analysis of redistribution between immigrants and
    people born in the United States within the American social security system. See also Chapter
    9 in Borjas (1990). Hammarstedt (2001) analyses immigrants in the Swedish national social in-
    surance system.

which can be viewed as publicly financed private goods. It is also possible to distinguish a part 4) consisting of public sector activities directly connected to immigrants.

When the cost of public sector goods is independent of the size of the population, and when their value for each resident of the country does not depend on the total number of people residing in the country (no crowding effects), these goods are generally referred to as 'public goods'. Common examples are expenses related to maintaining the royal family, diplomatic representation, defence and border control. However, it is not self-evident that these costs do not vary in accordance with the size of the population. Defence is a good example. Denmark is a member of NATO and contributes to NATO's common defence with forces. The contribution expected from a given country depends upon the size of the country's population. If the population of Denmark were twice its present size, NATO would expect a greater defence contribution, and defence expenses would probably be higher. Nevertheless, a certain degree of inertia is associated with this area. The same is also true of investments in infrastructure such as highways and bridges.

Another type of public sector activity is dependent in a more obvious way upon the size of the population. This is the case, for example, for expenses related to maintaining road networks. If the size of the population grows, more residential areas will be built, and an expanded infrastructure for residential areas (for example, local road networks) will be necessary.

A third category of public consumption can be tied to individuals. This is the case, for example, for education and health care. If there is an increase in the number of schoolchildren, costs will also rise, and it is easy to see the direct financial effect of the increase.

A fourth kind of public consumption is that which is provided specifically for immigrants, and whose costs can be directly related to the immigrants. In certain cases, these costs can be attributed to particular individuals, and sometimes they can be tied to the immigrants as a group. An example of an activity whose costs can be related to particular individuals would be instruction in the Danish language specifically for immigrants. Another example would be initiatives specially directed at pre-school and school-aged children of immigrants.[36] Public support of immigrant associations is an example of a cost that is difficult to relate to specific individuals, but which can be related to immigrants as a group. Measures such as these can be referred to as *immigrant* policy, as opposed to *immigration* policy, which is something altogether different. Immigration policy consists of measures aimed at regulating the number of immigrants who arrive and are permitted to remain in the country.

––––––––––––––––

36   For an example, see Mehlbye (1994).

It is very important to distinguish between immigrant policy – which is related to the fact that immigrants are living in a country and which is generally aimed at assisting immigrants in various ways – and immigration policy, which regulates the influx of immigrants to the country. The expenses related to dealing with people seeking asylum and to returning refugees who are not granted asylum in Denmark to their countries of origin are covered under border control activities, and form a part of immigration policy, but not of immigrant policy.

In some countries, the costs associated with a national debt are considerable.[37] The question is to whom these costs should be attributed – should they be counted as part of expenses related to immigrants as well as for the native population, or should they be distributed in another manner? The answer depends in part upon the dates involved. Assume that a country has a considerable national debt at the beginning of a given year, and that immigrants arrive in the country at the beginning of the same year. Their arrival does not influence the existing national debt, and the costs associated with the debt neither rise nor fall. On the other hand, an increase in debt-related expenditure should be counted if this is due to any increase in the national debt that occurs while immigrants are living in the country, and which is due to a situation where the amount of taxes paid by immigrants fails to cover the costs of transfers to those same immigrants and other expenditure on public sector activities related to their presence in the country. A problem with cross sectional studies can arise in this connection, as it is difficult to ensure accurate dating in the calculations.

2.2 The distribution of revenues and expenditures per individual

As regards the discussion of the various revenues and expenditure items within the public sector, it is clear that the most important principle is that expenditure should be tied to specific individuals as closely as possible. This is easy in the case of certain items – for instance, when information is available about who attends a particular school, who has been admitted to a hospital, and so on. It is even easier in the case of transfers, as a direct connection can most often be made. Sometimes this information is lacking, even in cases where individual-oriented public consumption is involved, and it then becomes necessary to work with general patterns, for example, in order to distribute expenditure evenly for all individuals in a particular age group. Certain kinds of expenditure cannot, as previously mentioned, even theoretically be related to specific individuals, even if the expenditure varies in accordance with the

---

37   See MaCurdy, Nechyba & Bhattacharya (1998) for an analysis.

number of individuals in the economy. In such cases, general patterns and averages are the only way forward.

The fact that not all expenditures can be tied to specific individuals can give rise to a particular problem if people do not always notify the authorities when they leave a country, and thus appear in records to be residing in the country even after they have moved. If all taxes, transfers and public sector expenditure could be directly tied to payments or the use of services, then this lag in the reporting of emigration would not constitute a problem. Now a greater or smaller portion of expenditure must be distributed on the basis of general patterns, while taxes can, in essence, be tied directly to individuals. For those who move out of the country tax revenues will fall, while some of the public sector expenditure remains in the calculations. This means that the estimates of net transfers to these immigrants and to immigrants as a group are too high. Even without this lag, incorrect estimates can be produced for individuals who emigrate during the year for which the net transfer is calculated. The problem with such lags and with emigration during the year under study increases the higher the rate of emigration, and the greater the lag in reporting emigration and the proportion of expenditure that is distributed based on general patterns.[38]

The way in which an analysis is carried out should depend upon the questions to be answered. The basic question in much of the discussion is: what effect does a marginal increase (or a non-marginal increase) in the number of immigrants moving to Denmark have on public sector finances? An alternative question is the following: what does the redistribution pattern between Danes and immigrants look like in a given year?

If one wishes to attempt to answer the first question, one solution might be to follow a particular cohort, such as all people who immigrated to Denmark in 1960, and then to examine the redistribution pattern between this particular group and the rest of the population for each year, and attempt to project what will happen in years to come. One could then repeat the analysis cohort by cohort. It is important not to limit the period of study for the respective cohorts in such a way as to distort the

---

38 According to a conversation with Anita Lange, Statistics Denmark, follow-up routines with respect to an individual's residence status are good in Denmark, and thus the problem is not especially serious. According to a study of the educational level of immigrants in Denmark carried out by Statistics Denmark (Mørkeberg 2000), 6,502 of 159,029 immigrants included in the survey were not possible to reach or had emigrated without notifying that they had done so. This indicates that there is a problem with unregistered emigration even in Denmark. In Sweden cases of failure to report emigration constitute between 3 and 10 per cent of the population of immigrants from non-Nordic countries. See Greijer (1995), (1996), (1997) and (1997a) and Nilsson (1995).

analysis. Children of immigrants must be included (second and third generation immigrants), in any case for a period of time that is long enough for any differences between the immigrant cohort and the native population to have disappeared (i.e. for the cohort to become assimilated).[39] Children born in marriages between immigrants and Danes must also be counted, even if this group should be distributed equally between the immigrant and native populations.

The type of study described above where cohorts are followed and projections are made requires a great deal of data, and useful information is generally only available for recent years. This means that, in practice, cohorts can be followed for only a few years. On the other hand, it is possible to construct artificial cohorts and to attempt to make assumptions that are as realistic as possible based on the study of cross sectional information.[40]

A typical feature of studies of cohorts (both real and artificial) is that the result is highly dependent on the age composition of the immigrants under study. In general, a large proportion of people who immigrate are of younger active age or the children of these immigrants. By contrast, relatively few are older (older but still active or over pension age). If one only examines those who have themselves immigrated (excluding children born after their parents have immigrated), then one examines a group of people who gradually grow older. If children (and future generations) are included, the age composition of the group gradually comes more and more to resemble that of the native population, if the fertility and mortality pattern is the same. Provided the immigrants find employment, we also see a net transfer from the immigrants for a number of years subsequent to their immigration, and that these transfers then gradually cease. What is emphasised in this type of model is that immigrants who are of younger active age when they arrive have already had their childhood and youth expenses paid in their country of origin, and that they arrive as members of an age group from which transfers generally occur to those who are below (children and youth) or above an active age (the elderly). An even clearer illustration of this type of redistribution is found in countries that have adopted a 'guest worker' system, and where immigrants only reside in the country for a year or a few years while they are of active age.

With respect to the problem of data, cross sectional investigation is the method

---

39   There are several studies of the integration of the first and second generations of immigrants but few of the third generation. Epstein and Lecker (2001) study integration of the first, second and third generation of immigrants in Israel. Maybe a somewhat surprising result is that the earnings of the third generation are higher than those of the first generation but lower than those of the second generation.

40   See, for example, Storesletten (1998) and Gustafsson & Larsson (1998, section 6) for two cohort-based analyses.

most frequently employed in studies of the fiscal effects of immigration. Such studies examine the occurrence of redistribution over the course of a year (or more) between the immigrants and the native population. It is important to include the children of immigrants. If they are not included, only a portion of the effects of the increase in population enters into the calculations. Data problems associated with this can arise in connection with the descendants of earlier groups of immigrants. A possible solution is to limit the investigation to a group of immigrants who arrived in the country after a particular year (after 1970, for example). The problem then is that one can generally see whatever redistribution occurs during the first decades after the immigration, but not after that (for example studying redistribution when people are 20–50 years old but not when they are older).

2.3 The public sector on different levels

When we refer to transfers carried out via the public sector, we generally ignore the fact that the public sector is divided into different, often highly independent, levels. In Scandinavian countries, we can generally distinguish between three or four levels – first the state level, then the regional level (county level), and finally the municipal level. A fourth level or form of organisation that often has a separate economy is the social insurance system or a part of that system. Immigration influences the different levels in different ways, depending upon the tax and fee system, rules for transfer payments, etc.

It may seem only to be a minor problem to add up the different levels of the public sector, and if a study of the totality of effects is all that is required, then proceeding in such a manner might be reasonable. Yet arguments can be made in favour of dividing the various entities that make up the public sector.

The first of these arguments is that results for the respective levels can influence behaviour. Let us imagine two different cases and assume that the total effect is the same in both cases: 1) in the first case, the state wins, while the municipality loses; 2) in the second case, the municipality wins, while the state loses. We cannot dismiss the possibility that the two types of results will influence the actions of the municipality with respect to measures that influence the number of immigrants who settle in the municipality. If, to take an extreme example, the municipalities must bear the expenses and the state reaps the benefits, the municipalities could feasibly attempt to direct immigrants towards other municipalities.[41]

---

41   There are examples in nineteenth century Sweden of municipalities attempting to move costly families into other municipalities by means of relocation assistance.

A second argument is that the system ought to take a neutral position to redistribution with respect to effects on people who live in different parts of the country. The overall level of immigration is determined by the state. In a country such as Denmark, a large number of newly arrived immigrants are refugees, and the rules that govern who will be accepted as refugees are established centrally (i.e. at the state level). Those who are granted permission to enter the country are thus accepted and must settle somewhere in the country. Finding acceptance in a given municipality can be more difficult if the distribution of expenses between the municipality and the state results in a situation where the municipality is responsible for a large portion of the expenses, while income (tax revenue) is received at the state level.

Both of these arguments indicate the fact that it is important to acquire knowledge about the actual distribution as well as to have a way of compensating those municipalities that accept refugees to provide them with reasonable incentives to do so.

The fact that the fiscal effects can actually vary from level to level has been demonstrated in investigations of immigrants in two states in the USA, California and New Jersey. These studies indicate a small net income for the Federal level but a net expenditure on the state and local levels.[42]

One Danish study sheds at least some light on the question.[43] The study deals with the Danish municipalities' net extra expenditure for immigrants in 1995 and is based on information from 23 municipalities. This net expenditure is primarily influenced by the fact that immigrants show a different demographic composition, but also by special provisions for immigrants as a group. The net expenditure amounts to 7,300 Danish *kroner* per immigrant (6,800 Danish *kroner* per refugee and 7,700 Danish *kroner* per immigrant defined as a non-refugee immigrant). No consideration has been taken either to taxes paid by immigrants (compared to those paid by the native population) or to the fact that this expenditure influences tax rate equalisation measures and also various contributions from the state to the municipality. It is thus not possible to form a complete picture of how the municipalities are influenced based on this particular study.

A report produced by the Danish Ministry of the Interior's Finance Committee deals with the present system of redistribution between different municipalities and counties, and attempts to calculate the effects of the presence of foreign citizens in a municipality on the municipality's expenditure.[44] In the present system of redistri-

---

42   See Clune (1998), Garvey & Espenshade (1998) and Smith & Edmonston (1997).
43   See Christoffersen & Mørch Andersen (1997).
44   See Indenrigsministeriet (1998), p. 293.

bution between municipalities, the number of foreigners from third-world countries – who, for the purposes of this system, include the citizens of all countries other than the Nordic countries, members of the European Union and North America[45] – are included as one of the factors that determine socially conditioned redistribution. In this redistribution system, the number of foreign citizens equals a factor, which represents 10 per cent of the socially conditioned redistribution. Since socially conditioned redistribution constitutes 20 per cent of the redistribution basis (most of it is dependent on age composition), this means that the foreign citizen factor is attributed a weighting of 2 per cent in the redistribution system as a whole. There is, in addition, a form of redistribution which is tied directly to the fact that foreign citizens of this group of countries reside in the municipality and which provides a subsidy of a particular amount per person. This amount varies according to age and the length of the period of residence in the country in the case of refugees (the longer this period, the lower the subsidy), and a certain low amount is also paid per asylum seeker. This type of subsidy amounts to a total of 4 billion Danish *kroner in* 1999.

The report also contains a regression analysis in which the actual expenditure in a municipality per resident – or per resident belonging to a particular (age)-group that is relevant to the type of expenditure in question – is explained by making use of certain variables, where the percentage of foreign residents from third-world countries is one of the factors. It appears that the effect of the number of foreign citizens on the level of expenditure is statistically significant in three areas: library and leisure-time expenditure, state school expenditure for students aged 7–16, and housing subsidy expenditure for people between 20–59. In all of these cases, expenditure is higher if the percentage of foreign residents is higher, which indicates that the redistribution that has taken place is supported by actual differences in expenditure (although it cannot be determined on the basis of this study whether the redistribution corresponds to the actual differences in costs).

The result of this investigation indicates the importance of carrying out further research in this area, in order to form a better basis for decision-making regarding the design of the redistribution system.

---

45   Citizens of countries such as Switzerland, Australia, New Zealand and Japan are in that system included among those who come from third-world countries.

Chapter 3

Immigration and the Public Sector: Experiences from Different Countries

A number of studies of the fiscal effects of immigration based on cross sectional analyses have been carried out in different countries. We will discuss studies from Denmark, Norway, Sweden, Germany, Italy, Spain, the United States, Australia and Canada.

Denmark

A Danish study of the fiscal effects of immigrants in 1995, produced by the Ministry of Economic Affairs, attempts to a very great extent to allocate both tax revenues and expenditure directly to individuals.[46] This should make the study more reliable than many others conducted in other countries, and also less sensitive to the issue of people leaving the country without being registered as having done so.

The total fiscal effects amount to DKK 1 billion *from* group 1 immigrants (immigrants from EU countries, Norway, Iceland, Switzerland, North America, Australia and New Zealand), DKK 11.3 billion *to* immigrants from group 2 countries (all other countries) and DKK 58.9 billion *from* the rest of the population. The figures per person over 18 are DKK +10,600, DKK -82,000 and DKK +15,000. A distinction is also made between those who are employed full time and those employed part time or not employed at all. The result shows that the fiscal transfers to group 2 immigrants go to individuals who are not employed full time, and that the total effect is governed to a great extent by the fact that the level of employment in this group is low.

With the help of a demographic model, Pedersen and Trier (2001) have calculated the tax rate necessary to finance the public expenditures in Denmark in the 21st century, given the rules of the social insurance system and given the present standard of public services. The result is that the tax rate has had to increase by 2.8 percentage units in the basis alternative. If the immigration increases by 5,000 people per year compared to the assumption in the basis alternative, the tax rate has to increase by 0.31 percentage units more than in that alternative. The low employment rate among immigrants is the explanation for the tax burden being higher in that alter-

---

46   See Ministry of Economic Affairs (1997) and Christensen (1998).

native. In another calculation all immigrants are assumed to arrive at the age of 17 (just below the age for active age) the effect is smaller, 0.09 percentage units more than the basis alternative, but it is still negative.

Norway

Larsen and Bruce (1998) have carried out a study of redistribution via the public sector in Norway. Their results indicate a significant redistribution to refugee immigrants, while there is a smaller transfer from other immigrants.[47] The factor that to a great extent determines these results is the poor labour market situation especially for refugee immigrants. If immigrants were employed at the same levels as the rest of the population in the same age group, the net transfer to refugees would fall significantly, and the net fiscal transfer from other immigrants would rise sharply.

Sweden

A number of studies of the fiscal effects of immigration based on cross sectional analyses have been carried out in Sweden. The experience in Sweden is that results have changed over time, as immigration itself has changed from being an immigration of workers to primarily refugee immigration, and as the Swedish economy has also undergone considerable transformation.

A study of labour immigration during the 1960s from four countries (Finland, Germany, Italy, and Yugoslavia), where the fiscal calculations relate to the year 1969, indicates a considerable net transfer from the immigrants to the rest of the population. See Wadensjö (1973). Of decisive importance for the results of this study was the fact that the immigrants who were studied had a very high level of labour force participation.

A study of immigrants in the 1970s suggests that at that time there was still a net transfer from the immigrants, but that it was considerably smaller. See Ekberg (1983).

Later studies show a fairly considerable net transfer to the immigrants. See Ekberg (1998) for a review of different studies. According to a study by Gustafsson & Österberg (2001)[48], this reversal occurred in the early 1990s, at the same time that unemployment quickly rose in Sweden. According to a study by Ekberg (1999) the net transfer amounted to 0.9 per cent of the GDP in 1991 and 2.0 per cent of the GDP in 1994. The large difference between the two years is explained mainly by the

---

47   The groups included in the study are primarily first and second-generation immigrants in Norway.

48   Also published as Chapter 1 in Österberg (2000).

downturn of the Swedish economy in this period, and also that there was a large influx of refugees who were not able to get jobs in the recession period. In Ekberg & Andersson (1995) the total net transfer from the public sector to the immigrants in 1991 and 1994 is dispersed on the state, the county councils and the municipalities. The state is responsible for the main part of the net transfer to the immigrants, 90 per cent in 1991 and 82 per cent in 1994.

A study by Storesletten (1998) shows that the age at which immigrants arrive, and their employment rate, is of utmost importance for the fiscal impact. Gustafsson and Österberg (2001) analyse individual net transfers to the public sector. For that study they have been able to use individual data on public transfers. To calculate the taxes paid they have used individual data on earnings and on public transfers. Other public expenditures have either been allocated according to age or the same amount for everyone. The result is that net transfer to the public sector is influenced by age, family status and education but also by country of origin and the length of stay in Sweden.

Germany

A study of immigrants and the fiscal impact in Germany by Bonin, Raffelhüschen & Walliser (2000) uses survey data in a general accounting framework.[49] The main conclusion is that the net contribution of prospective immigrants is positive if their fiscal behaviour is similar to that observed in cross-section data from 1996. Half of the positive effect depends on the favourable age composition of the immigrants, half of it on the fact that immigration raises the size of future cohorts (and there is redistribution from future to present cohorts).

Italy

Based on two surveys, Moscarola (2001) has calculated the net transfer to the public sector for Italians and immigrants. As separate information for immigrants has not been available, other information sources have been used to adjust the values for the survey of the total population so as to obtain estimates of taxes, transfers and public expenditures for immigrants. From this information, the pattern of net transfer to the public sector for Italians and immigrants according to age is calculated for 1998. From that, the net present value profile has been calculated for immigrants arriving at different ages (from 15 years of age). The net transfer to the public sector is

---

49   See also Bonin (2001).

positive if the stay is five years or longer (if shorter than five years the initial costs for adjustment leads to a negative result for the public sector).

Spain

Collado, Iturbe-Ormaetye and Valera (2001) have studied the fiscal impact of immigration to Spain in a generational framework. They have utilized information from population projections and age-profiles for taxes and transfers and other expenditures based on different surveys (for Spain and in one instance another country) for the generational accounts. The calculations are made for three alternative immigration scenarios: a net emigration of 30,000 a year (the present level), 0, and 100,000. An increased immigration substantially lowers the burden on future natives. Even if the immigrants are paying less in taxes due to the fact that they earn less, the gain on the expenditure side is more important. The favourable age distribution of the immigrants leads to the public expenditures for the group being relatively low.

United States

A review of American studies published in 1998[50] shows that the fiscal effects of immigration are negative in all cases. However, all of these studies lack important details of the precise accounting for expenditure and income. This makes them difficult to interpret. Studies carried out within the framework of the National Research Council's recent comprehensive report on the effects of immigration, and which are considerably more thorough as regards the system of accounting for expenditure and income, still produce similar results.[51] The net effect is positive on the Federal level, but negative on the state and the local level. The results received in the studies reviewed by MaCurdy are highly sensitive to the definition of the immigrant population. The studies are based on immigrant households. Such studies tend to give more negative impacts, as the people included are first generation immigrants as well as second-generation immigrants living in the household of their parents. Most of those second-generation immigrants are young, below active age.

Lee and Miller (2000) also present results from a longitudinal model with detailed demographic forecasts included for the second and later generations. Predictions are

---

50 MaCurdy, Nechyba & Bhattacharya (1998). See Simon (1984) for an early study of the fiscal effects of immigration for the US.

51 See Clune (1998), Garvey & Espenshade (1998), Lee & Miller (1998) and Smith & Edmonston (1997).

made for the development of the tax, transfer and public services systems. Using this model the effects on the net present value is calculated for immigrants arriving in 1998 for different time horizons. If the time horizon is 30 years or more the net effect is positive, in other cases negative. The effects are divided between the state/local (negative) and the federal level (positive). The effects are also calculated for a part of the federal sector, the social insurance system (OASDI). The net present value is positive for this part of the public sector. The effects for the federal budget and especially for OASDI, given the present size of immigration, are not large enough to have a significant impact. See Lee (2001a).

Auerbach & Oreopoulos (1999, 1999a) analyse the fiscal impact of immigration in a generational accounting framework for the United States. The results vary with the assumption regarding the distribution between present and future generations. The effects of immigration are more positive for the public sector if the redistribution goes from younger to older generations. The sign of the effect differs depending on how large a part of the costs for public consumption and investment is assumed to vary with the size of the population.

Storesletten (2000) finds in a study of the fiscal effects of immigration to the United States that the effects are highly sensitive to the age and skills of immigrants upon arrival in the United States. The main result is that immigration can have a largely positive impact for the fiscal policy, but that the effect is highly dependent on the composition of the immigrants who enter the country.

Australia

Ablett (1999) analyses the effects of immigration on the public sector in Australia in a generational framework. The main conclusion is that immigration is likely to make a substantial net positive contribution to the Australian public sector. It should be noted that the calculations build on the assumption of the same average payment and benefit level for immigrants and nonimmigrants who belong to the same age/gender cohort. It may be argued that differences in payment and benefit levels between immigrants and natives are less important in Australia than in European countries like Denmark.

Canada

Akbari (1989, 1991) studied the fiscal effects of immigrants who arrived in Canada in 1979 or earlier, based on the 1981 Canadian census of population (the information is for 1980). The fiscal effects are calculated for four different groups of origin: 1) United States, 2) United Kingdom, 3) Western Europe, and 4) Asia, Africa and

South and Central America. The net present value for the public sector is calculated for a representative immigrant household arriving in 1980. The discount rate is set to 2.5 per cent. The net contribution is positive for all four immigrant groups – highest for those arriving from the United Kingdom and lowest for those arriving from Western Europe. To put the results in perspective it should be mentioned that most immigrants to Canada are economic migrants or relatives of earlier economic migrants, and not refugees, and that the Canadian migration policy favours highly skilled and highly educated migrants.[52]

A short summary of the international experiences

The fiscal impact of immigration varies between the countries studied and also within each country depending on the time period that was covered and the method that was used. Common to all the different studies is that the immigrants have a population structure that has a positive fiscal impact. On the other hand, in most cases the employment rate and the earnings are lower for immigrants than for natives, which leads to lower tax payments and higher social transfers to the immigrants than to natives among those of active age. It means that in most countries there is one factor, the age structure, giving a positive fiscal impact, and one factor, the employment conditions, giving a negative impact. In some cases the first factor is the most important, in other cases the second factor. The results are also dependent on whether the calculations cover the first generation, the first generation and the childhood and youth of the second generation, or the first and second generation (or even more generations). The important lesson is that the results differ greatly between countries, depending on the choice of method. It means that it is important to make a careful study of the country that is the focus of interest, in our case Denmark.

---

52   See DeVoretz & Laryea (1999) for an analysis of the Canadian immigration policy.

Chapter 4
The Data

The study presented in this book is based on data from the Ministry of Economic Affairs' Law Model.[53] The database contains detailed information on income, taxes, transfers, and public consumption for 1/30 (3.3 per cent) of the population living in Denmark. A new model population is created every year. There is also information regarding demographic variables including whether a person is an immigrant or has a parent who is. The database also has information on employment status.

This study builds on detailed information from the Law Model covering average values for many different items for five years – 1991 and 1995-98 – for various groups (including groups of immigrants). For four years, 1995-1998, information covering the net transfer on the individual level combined with some other variables has been used for the analysis. For three years – 1996, 1997 and 1998 – data on individuals aged 18 years and older, with information for the children included as part of the net transfer for their parents, has been used. For 1995 and 1998 information on the net transfer for all, independent of age – not only those 18 years and older – has also been available, which makes it easier to see how the net transfer varies over the life cycle. There is information on demographic variables – age, gender, family type, immigration status (classified after country of birth and country of birth of the parents, and year of arrival) – on net transfers between the individual and the public sector and on the individual employment rate. Information on the country of origin is divided into two categories: Western and non-Western countries.[54]

The data sets for 1995, 1996 and 1998 contain some extra variables. For 1995, 1996 and 1998 information on different types of income on the individual level has been available for the analysis, and for 1995 and 1998 also information on the household composition. For 1996 information on how the net transfer to the public sector is divided between the state, the counties, the municipalities and the unemployment insurance scheme is included. In addition to information on the individual level, more detailed information on the composition of the items has been available on the group level.

---

53 See Ministry of Economic Affairs (2000) for a presentation of the database. Knudsen, Larsen & Pedersen (1998) and Linderoth (1999) give detailed presentations of the structure of the public sector and of the tax system in Denmark.

54 See Table 4.2 for information on how the groups are defined.

For Chapter 8 the analysis builds on a panel for 1995 and 1998 with the same set of variables applying to the data sets for 1995 and 1998.

4.1 The variables in the database

Table 4.1 shows the variables included in the different registers used in the estimations based on individual observations. From those variables it has been possible to construct various other variables.

The major part of the public sector's costs and revenues are distributed on individuals in the Law Model.[55] The direct personal income taxes are ascribed to the individuals who are paying them, and the indirect taxes are distributed on the individuals in proportion to their disposable income. Income transfers are referred to those individuals who receive them. The main part of public consumption is either distributed after information on actual use (for example school, health care, and old age care) or evenly divided on the population. Also public investment (for example road investments) are evenly distributed on the whole population (both Danes and immigrants). The public sector costs, which are not distributed on individuals and therefore not included in the Law Model, are such costs that are assumed to be independent of the size of the population. Some examples are central state administration, defence, and some subsidies to the private sector (especially agriculture). In 1995 the total public expenditure was 605,200 million Danish *kroner*. Of this expenditure 397,600 was distributed on individuals. Of the taxes 446,100 million out of 489,900 million was distributed on individuals.[56]

The variable net transfer to the public sector is calculated for each individual as the difference between the taxes ascribed to the individual and the sum of income transfers and public consumption and investment ascribed to the same individual. Compared to an analysis by the Ministry of Economic Affairs[57] in 1995 there is one important difference as regards the items included in the calculation. In the analysis presented here, the costs for refugees in the period before they know if they will obtain refugee status or not, are excluded. We consider those costs as a part of the regulation of immigration and as such part of the border control costs.[58] In the data

---

55 See Ministry of Economic Affairs (1997) pp. 188-200 for a presentation of how the different items are assigned to individuals.

56 See Ministry of Economic Affairs (1997). See also le Maire & Scheuer (2001) for a detailed presentation of what is and what is not distributed on individuals in the 1998 Law Model.

57 See Ministry of Economic Affairs (1997) and Indenrigsministeriet (1999).

58 For a more detailed discussion see Wadensjö (1999). The costs involved before decisions were taken to allow the immigrant to stay or not were 546 million *kroner* in 1991, 2,433 million *kroner* in 1995, 2,273 million *kroner* in 1996, and 1,290 million *kroner* in 1997 (in current prices for each year).

TABLE 4.1.

Variables in the individual information based part of the study

VARIABLES	DESCRIPTION	YEAR
Gender	Male/female	1995, 1996, 1997, 1998
Age	Age in years	1995, 1996, 1997, 1998
Year of birth		1995, 1996, 1997, 1998
Family status	Marital and parental status	1995, 1996, 1997, 1998
Children	No. of own children	1995, 1996, 1997, 1998
Children in household	No. of children in the household	1995, 1998
Adults in household	No. of adults in the household	1995, 1998
Country of origin	Grouped as Denmark, Western country or non-Western country*	1995, 1996, 1997, 1998
Year of immigration	The year of latest immigration**	1995, 1996, 1997, 1998
Date of immigration	Year-month-day of latest immigration**	1995, 1996, 1998
Length of stay	No. of years since latest immigration	1995, 1996, 1997, 1998
Employment rate	Ranges from 0-100 where 100=full-time and full-year employment***	1995, 1996, 1997, 1998
Earnings	Annual earnings	1995, 1996, 1998
Income from labour	The sum of earnings and income as self-employed	1995, 1996, 1998
Income tax	The sum of income taxes and fees to unemployment insurance scheme	1995, 1996, 1998
Income from interest		1995, 1996, 1998
Expenses from interest		1995, 1996, 1998
Disposable income	Total income (subsidies included) minus taxes, expenses from interest, fees to unemployment insurance scheme, child maintenance and pension fees	1995, 1996, 1998
Disposable income, household	The household's total disposable income	1995, 1998
Net transfer	Net transfer to public sector	1995, 1996, 1997, 1998
Net transfer, state sector	Net transfer to state sector only	1996
Net transfer, municipalities	Net transfer to municipalities only	1996
Net transfer, counties	Net transfer to counties only	1996
Net transfer, unemployment insurance scheme	Net transfer to unemployment insurance scheme only	1996
Net transfer, sum	The sum of the net transfers to municipalities and counties	1996
Net transfer, not distributed	Net transfer that does not fit in classifications above	1996

TABEL 4.1 continued

* Western countries are EU countries, Norway, Switzerland, Iceland, North America, Australia and New Zealand; non-Western countries are all other countries. It is also possible to identify those individuals who have one Danish parent and one from a Western or non-Western country.

** Exact number of years is available only for those who have immigrated in the last ten years (for the 1998 sample information is available on year of arrival for a part of those who arrived in 1970-1985 and for all who have arrived 1986 or later). The reason for the difference is that previously the information covering the year of immigration was deleted for those who had immigrated more than ten years earlier. From 1999 this rule was abolished but already in 1998 some information on earlier years was added.

*** There is a change in the calculation of the employment rate from 1997 on. It leads to a calculated employment rate slightly below 100 per cent for many individuals, even if they have been full-year and full-time employed. As the values differ only slightly from 100, it leads to problems only when we especially study those who are full-year and full-time employed. We have in those cases set an employment rate of 98 per cent as the lower limit to be counted for that group.

from the Ministry of Economic Affairs for 1998 those costs are not included so it has not been necessary to adjust the figures for that year.

The basic principles for the Law Model have been the same for all of the five years covered by this study. However, there may have been some variations as to what extent it has been possible to attribute the transfers and other public expenditure to individuals. One example is that costs for brief or extended care in a hospital are based on individual information in 1998, but on an average of the costs for all aged 18 and over for 1997 and earlier years.[59] It means that small differences between the years should be interpreted with care. Details on how taxes, transfers and public consumption and investments are distributed on individuals in 1995 are presented in a report of the Ministry of Economic Affairs (1997, pp. 188-203).

4.2 The sample for the study

The Law Model contains many observations covering almost 140,000 people aged 18 or over every year. The large sample means that quite a few immigrants are included in the database – almost 3,000 from Western countries and more than 5,000 from non-Western countries. In spite of the large number of immigrants the number of observations is rather small for studying certain groups of immigrants, for example immigrants belonging to a certain age group.

Table 4.2 contains information on the size of the various groups, both Danes and those who have an immigrant background, and who are 18 years and older. The age limit of 18 years in this table is because the data set in all years except 1995 and 1998 includes the net transfer to children under 18 years of age to their parents. For 1998 the values are calculated in two ways: 1) with the net transfer to children 17 years or younger as part of the parents' net transfer and 2) with all, also those 17 years and

---

59 See Ministry of Economic Affairs (2001).

TABLE 4.2.

Number of individuals included in the study who are 18 years or older

GROUP	1991	1995	1996	1997	1998
Danish population (excluding those with one immigrant parent)	128,740	128,972	128,788	128,859	128,899
Second generation – one Danish parent and one immigrant parent from Western countries	1,194	1,447	1,468	1,474	1,551
Second generation – one Danish parent and one immigrant parent from non-Western countries	231	356	328	316	395
Immigrants from Western countries	2,410	2,673	2,789	2,702	2,939
Second generation – parents from Western countries	210	216	248	245	237
Immigrants from non-Western countries	3,312	4,396	4,882	5,097	5,407
Second generation – parents from non-Western countries	82	167	216	234	273
Total	136,179	138,227	138,719	138,927	139,701

Note: Western countries are EU countries, Norway, Switzerland, Iceland, North America, Australia and New Zealand; non-Western countries are all other countries.

younger, as separate individuals. For the other years, information is available for those aged 17 years or younger but only if they pay taxes; there is no information about public expenditure. In the data set their expenditures are a part of the expenditures attributed to their parents. For 1996 and 1997 those aged 17 years or younger have not been included in the calculations based on individual data. However, their tax payments are included in the aggregate data presented for each population group. The tax payments are small for those aged 17 or younger. For all those aged 17 or younger the taxes paid were less than 2,000 *kroner* per person in 1996 as well as in 1997. To make the figures comparable, the same calculation has been made for 1998 as for earlier years, but of course in other calculations the information for those 17 years and younger in the 1998 sample has also been used.

In Table 4.2 individuals are referred to different groups, depending on where they were born and where their parents were born (Denmark, Western countries, non-Western countries). Two comments should be made to the definitions. People who were born abroad but who have Danish parents are counted as belonging to the Danish group (this group includes adopted children and children of Danes who have been working in another country but later returned to Denmark). There are a few people with one parent from a Western country and one parent from a non-Western country. They have been classified after the origin of their mother.

TABLE 4.3.

Number of children in the 1998 sample 17 years or younger

GROUP	ACCORDING TO PARENTS' NATIONALITY	ACCORDING TO OWN NATIONALITY
Danish population (excluding those with one immigrant parent)	32,457	32,493
Second generation – one Danish parent and one immigrant parent from Western countries	539	1,115
Second generation – one Danish parent and one immigrant parent from non-Western countries	80	768
Immigrants from Western countries	700	165
Second generation – parents from Western countries	77	127
Immigrants from non-Western countries	3,013	983
Second generation – parents from non-Western countries	36	1,796
Total	36,902	37,447

Note: Western countries are EU countries, Norway, Switzerland, Iceland, North America, Australia and New Zealand; non-Western countries are all other countries.

The table shows that the groups who have foreign backgrounds are considerably larger in 1998 than in 1991. It is especially so for two groups – second generation immigrants from non-Western countries whose numbers are more than three times greater in 1998 than in 1991, and immigrants from non-Western countries whose numbers have increased by more than 60 per cent in the same period. Even the groups with one Danish parent and one parent born in another country had grown considerably between 1991 and 1995, although the number did not increase much between 1995 and 1998. The increase in the number of first and second-generation immigrants from Western countries is much smaller.

When the groups increase in size the estimates will be more accurate. The reliability of results will increase as information from the different years is included and combined.

Table 4.2 only gives figures for those aged 18 and over. For those 17 years of age or younger it is possible to classify them in the same way as their parents or to make an independent classification. If the costs of children are attributed to the parents the first classification method is used, if the children are included as separate individuals the second method is used. The number of children in 1998 in the different nationality groups according to the two methods is shown in Table 4.3.

A comparison of the total value according to the columns shows a difference. This difference can be explained by the fact that not all people 17 years or younger are included in the column for children according to parents' nationality. Those not included – 545 in total – are those already married, those who already have their own children, and those who live outside the family for other reasons, for example in institutions.

A comparison also shows that there are large differences in the composition of the groups according to the two principles. The reason for that is that most children of the first generation belong to the second generation of immigrants (they were born in Denmark). According to the parents' nationality (first column) they are counted as first generation immigrants, but according to their own nationality (second column) they are counted as second generation immigrants.

4.3 The calculation of the employment rate and the earnings variable

The employment rate is an important variable in many of the analyses in this book. An individual's employment rate varies between 0 and 100 per cent. To be counted as having an employment rate of 100 per cent, a person should have worked fulltime during the entire year. There are some problems regarding the definition of full-time. The working hours are calculated by using payment for the ATP pension scheme. Since 1993 a person who has 27 or more working hours a week has to pay a whole fee and is counted as working full-time in the Law Model.[60] A person who works at least 18 hours, but less than 27 hours, pays two-thirds of the full fee and is counted as having an employment rate of two-thirds (of course given that the person works the entire year). Those who work at least 9 hours but less than 18 hours pay one-third of the full fee and are counted as working one-third of full-time.[61] Those working less than 9 hours a week do not pay any ATP-fee and are not counted as employed. Before 1993 the hour limits were 30, 20 and 10 hours. It probably means that the employment rate for 1991 is underestimated compared to those for 1995, 1996 and 1998, as the change in the working week from 40 hours to 37 (proportionally for those working part-time) was gradual and mainly phased in before 1991.

---

60 The ATP-fee is also paid if a person is unemployed or on sick leave, but such periods are not included in the calculation of the employment rate.

61 Full-time work in Denmark is 37 hours a week. The full-time working week changed gradually from 40 to 37 in the period 1987 to 1992. Full time and full year, excluding the vacation period and public holidays, entails 1,692.5 hours a year. This figure is used in the calculation of the hourly wage rate.

Those who are self-employed, and the wife or husband who works in their family business are counted as having an employment rate of 100 per cent if the income is the same or higher than the maximal benefit level in the unemployment insurance. If the income for the self-employed is below that level and non-negative, the employment rate is proportionally reduced. For the self-employed with a negative income from that activity the employment rate is set to zero. For those who are part-time self-employed and part-time in someone else's employ, the two employment rates are added, but the employment rate is never set higher than 100.

The method of calculation of working hours means that it will not be correctly estimated for a number of people. For quite a few it will be an overestimation. People with long part-time work (for example 30 hours a week) will be counted as working full-time. Most likely more women than men will be wrongly classified in that way. The lower limit of 9 hours probably means that young people who are combining high school or university studies with odd jobs are wrongly counted as having an employment rate of 0. It is also not possible to see if people are working more than the full time of 37 hours a week with this method. Another problem is that those aged 67 or older do not pay an ATP-fee and therefore we do not know their employment rate.

The uncertainties in the calculations of the working week and the resulting uncertainties in calculations of the employment rate also mean that the calculation of the hourly wage by using information on the earnings and employment rate will be uncertain.

There is a special problem with the database, in that one group of foreign experts who stay in Denmark for a short time are taxed according to specific, favourable rules, meaning that 25 per cent of their earnings are exempted from taxation (see Skatteministeriet (2001)). To a very high extent, such people come from Western countries. The total number of people with that form of tax reduction has increased in the period covered by the present study. There were 103 in 1991; 744 in 1995; 752 in 1996; 1,167 in 1997; and 1,275 in 1998. In the 1998 sample of the Law Model it is possible to see how many have this specific type of tax reduction. The number was 36 (which, multiplied by 30, means c. 1,080 in the total population – somewhat lower than the actual number). 31 of the 36 were from Western countries, three from non-Western countries and two were Danes (who had lived outside Denmark for long periods).

This group causes problems in the calculations. The reason for this is that while they, as individuals, are included in the sample, up until 1998 their earnings, taxes paid, and ATP-fees were not included. The missing ATP-fees result in their being registered as not employed. It means that we get a number of Western immigrants with a low employment rate, low earnings and low tax payments when in fact the reverse is true. From 1998 this problem is solved and the information regarding earnings, taxes, and employment should be correct even for the 'expert group'.

Another similar problem is that those who receive their earnings from abroad do not pay ATP-fees and therefore are registered with an employment rate of 0. Also this group probably consists mainly of immigrants from Western countries.

4.4 A unique data base

In the preceding section we noted problems in connection with some variables in the database. The types of problems described are not uncommon for data taken from registers originally constructed for other purposes. However, it should be noted that the problems are only minor and that it is possible to handle them in this and other studies. The Law Model is a unique database that makes it possible to analyse various aspects of the public sector and also labour market issues. To our knowledge no database exists with the same quality and number of observations in other countries. It means that studies based on the Law Model are of great interest, even for other countries in the sense that is possible to answer more specific questions.

Chapter 5

The Labour Market, the Demographic Structure and Redistribution in the 1990s

The main theme of this book is the redistribution between immigrants and the public sector. In this chapter we will present the overall picture of the redistribution between immigrants and the public sector. This chapter is a follow-up study of three earlier studies of the aggregate fiscal effects of immigrants. The first by the Ministry of Economic Affairs, covered 1995.[62] Wadensjö (1999) covered 1991, 1995 and 1996 and Wadensjö (2000a) added data from 1997. This chapter adds corresponding information for 1998. As public expenditure and taxes paid are dependent on the employment situation and the demographic structure of the group, this chapter starts with two sections on the labour market situation among the immigrants and their demographic structure. The influences of those variables on the net transfers will be analysed in more detail in later chapters.

5.1 Immigrants and the labour market in the 1990s

In the preceding studies the redistribution was analysed in four years – 1991, 1995, 1996 and 1997. In this study we cover one more year – 1998. The labour market situation differs between the five years. This is seen, for example, if we follow the development of unemployment. The unemployment rate increased gradually from 1987 to a peak value in 1993. From that year the unemployment rate has gradually declined. In 1991, the first year covered in this study, the unemployment rate was increasing. On the other hand in 1995, the second year of this study, the unemployment rate was declining. The unemployment rate was slightly lower for the Danish population in 1995 than in 1991 but the unemployment rate among immigrants was somewhat higher in 1995 than in 1991. This is the case both for immigrants from Western and from non-Western countries.

The unemployment rate has gradually declined since 1995 for all three groups. For non-immigrants the unemployment rate is the lowest since the 1970s, as it is for Western immigrants for the period in which we have information (from 1984). For non-Western immigrants the unemployment is the lowest since the mid-1980s.

---

62   See Ministry of Economic Affairs (1997) and Christensen (1998).

TABLE 5.1.

Unemployment in Denmark among those aged 16-66 in 1991 and 1995-2000. Per cent

GROUP	1991	1995	1996	1997	1998	1999	2000
Danes	9.9	9.6	8.3	7.5	6.0	5.1	4.8
Immigrants from Western countries	13.3	13.9	11.9	10.9	8.4	7.3	6.8
Immigrants from non-Western countries	33.6	35.9	31.7	28.6	24.1	19.7	17.0

Note: Western countries are EU countries, Norway, Switzerland, Iceland, North America, Australia and New Zealand; non-Western countries are all other countries.

Source: See Appendix Table 3.2 in Chapter 3 in Viby Mogensen & Matthiessen (2000) and Schultz-Nielsen et al. (2001) and information from Rockwool Foundation Research Unit.

In Table 5.1 the unemployment rate is shown for those years covered by this study and also for 1999. The table shows that the unemployment rate was much lower in 1997 and 1998 than the preceding years and also that it continued to decline in 1999. In 1999 it was especially the unemployment rate for non-Western immigrants which declined.

Information on the unemployment rate alone, however, gives too positive a picture of the development of the labour market situation for immigrants in the Danish labour market. This is especially so for immigrants from non-Western countries. For this group the labour force participation rate declined considerably between 1995 and 1997 in spite of the improvement of the general economic situation in Denmark. See Table 5.2. Between 1995 and 1996 the decline in labour force participation was so large that it meant that the employment rate – measured as the share employed of those in active age – also declined. The employment rate measured in this way increased somewhat between 1996 and 1997. The development of employment for non-Western immigrants was more positive from 1997 to 1999. The labour force participation increased somewhat at the same time as the unemployment rate declined strongly.[63]

In this section of the chapter we will also give some information on the development of the average employment rate for the groups included in this study. Table 5.3 shows that the employment rate is very low for non-Western immigrants.[64] It

---

63 Rosholm et al. (2000) show that the development of employment for immigrants in Denmark and Sweden is similar in the period 1985-1995.

64 The figures for 1991 in Table 5.3 and 5.4 are higher than those presented in Wadensjö (1999) and Wadensjö (2000a). The reason for this is a correction in the calculations of the employment rates for the self-employed. The employment rate is probably still too low in 1991 compared to the rates in 1995-1998. This is due to the change in the rules for calculating ATP-fees from 1993, which constitute the basis for the calculation of the employment rates. See Chapter 4.

TABLE 5.2.

Labour force participation in Denmark among those aged 16-66 years in 1991 and 1995-2000. Per cent

Group	1991	1995	1996	1997	1998	1999	2000
Danes	80.4	79.6	78.8	78.7	79.0	78.9	79.0
Immigrants from Western countries	69.0	67.8	66.2	65.8	65.3	64.9	65.6
Immigrants from non-Western countries	57.3	55.0	50.1	49.2	50.2	51.2	51.1

Note: Western countries are EU countries, Norway, Switzerland, Iceland, North America, Australia and New Zealand; non-Western countries are all other countries.

Source: See Appendix Table 3.1 in Chapter 3 in Viby Mogensen & Matthiessen (2000) and Schultz-Nielsen et al. (2001) and information from Rockwool Foundation Research Unit.

increased somewhat in 1996, 1997 and 1998, but not very much. There are large variations in the employment rate among second generation immigrants from non-Western countries. One explanation is that the group is small and its age structure rapidly changes so it is difficult to draw any strong conclusions from the variations.

We will also study differences according to length of stay in Denmark for non-

TABLE 5.3.

Average rate of employment (full-time and full-year employment = 100) for the years 1991, 1995, 1996, 1997 and 1998 among those 18 years and older

GROUP	1991	1995	1996	1997	1998
Danish population (excluding those who have one immigrant parent)	52	54	54	55	56
Danish population (including those who have one immigrant parent)	52	54	54	55	56
Second generation – one Danish parent and one immigrant parent from a Western country	57	60	60	60	62
Second generation – one Danish parent and one immigrant parent from a non-Western country	50	54	49	51	55
Second generation – parents from Western countries	49	50	52	59	51
Immigrants from Western countries	42	40	43	41	43
Second generation – parents from non-Western countries	42	28	44	37	40
Immigrants from non-Western countries	27	22	25	27	31
Total	52	52	53	53	54

Note: Western countries are EU countries, Norway, Switzerland, Iceland, North America, Australia and New Zealand; non-Western countries are all other countries. For 1995 we have results from two independent samples. The differences between the values produced by the two samples are small. The numbers are from the data set used for the individual calculations.

TABLE 5.4.

Average rate of employment (full-time and full-year employment = 100) per person from non-Western countries according to length of stay in Denmark for the years 1991, 1995, 1996, 1997 and 1998 among those 18 years and older

LENGTH OF STAY	1991	1995	1996	1997	1998
Less than one year	3	3	5	5	11
1-3 years	14	14	11	15	24
3-5 years	21	19	17	15	22
5-7 years	25	23	20	23	26
7-10 years	26	27	25	28	30
10 years or more	37	35	36	38	39
Second generation	42	35	44	37	40
Total	27	25	26	28	31

Note: Western countries are EU countries, Norway, Switzerland, Iceland, North America, Australia and New Zealand; non-Western countries are all other countries. For 1995 we have results from two independent samples. The differences between the values produced by the two samples are small. The numbers are from the data set used for the individual calculations.

Western immigrants, see Table 5.4. The pattern is the expected one since those who have lived in Denmark for a longer period have a much higher employment rate than those who have lived in Denmark only a few years. However, compared to the Danish population also those who have been in Denmark ten years or more have a low employment rate. There is a positive development between 1997 and 1998 for those who have only lived in Denmark a short time. However, it is still low, only 24 per cent for those who have been in Denmark for 1-3 years.

As we have information on the employment rate and earnings it is possible to calculate a wage rate.[65] As mentioned in Chapter 4, the employment rate does not give an exact number of hours worked in a year so the calculated wage rates should be interpreted with care. The wage rate is of interest since not only the number of hours worked influences the tax paid and the transfers received but also the wage rate. Figure 5.1-5.3 shows the distribution of the hourly wage rate for the Danish population, immigrants from Western countries and immigrants from non-Western countries. Note that the scale is adjusted to the size of the groups and that those with an hourly wage rate of more than 500 *kroner* are excluded.

The shape of the wage structure is similar for the groups, but the average wage differs between them. The wage rate is highest for the immigrants from the Western

---

65   For studies of the wages of immigrants in Denmark see Husted et al. (2000, 2000a).

countries and lowest for those from the non-Western countries, with the wage rate for the Danish group somewhere in between. The pattern is the same if we only take those with an employment rate of 100 and make separate figures for men and women. The wage level is higher, but the order of the three groups is the same when the wage rates are compared. And, as expected, men have higher wage rates than women. The average hourly wage for those with an employment rate of 100 is 168.64 Danish *kroner* for Danish men, 179.52 for men from Western countries and 143.58 for men from non-Western countries. The corresponding values for women are 136.91, 150.55 and 128.10.

In countries that have minimum wage laws, you would expect the groups who have a weaker position in the labour market to have a 'spike' in wage distribution (i.e. that many would have just the minimum wage). In Denmark there is no minimum wage law but on the other hand the trade unions may act in such a way so that the outcome is more or less the same as in the case of the minimum wage law. However, we cannot find such 'spikes' for any of the groups.

FIGURE 5.1.

The structure of hourly wage rate among Danes in 1998 (in Danish *kroner*)

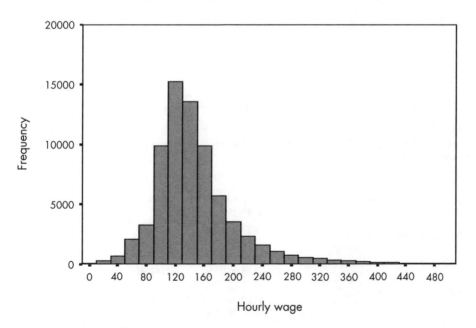

Note: Number of observations: 71,955, average hourly wage: 147.52, standard deviation 59.38. Only those aged 18-65 with an hourly wage larger than zero and equal to or less than 500 kroner are included (around 1 per cent have an hourly wage of 500 kroner or more). Those with income as self-employed are excluded.

FIGURE 5.2.

The structure of hourly wage rate among immigrants from Western countries in 1998 (in Danish *kroner*)

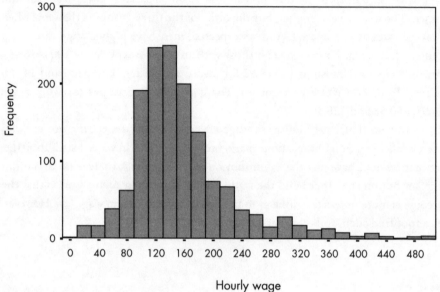

Hourly wage

Note: Number of observations: 1,478, average hourly wage: 158.23, standard deviation 71.98. Only those aged 18-65 with an hourly wage larger than zero and equal to or less than 500 kroner are included (around 1 per cent have an hourly wage of 500 kroner or more). Those with income as self-employed are excluded.

TABLE 5.5.

Average hourly wages in 1995, 1996 and 1998 (Amounts in 1998 prices in parentheses)

GROUP	1995	1996	1998
Danish population (excluding those who have one immigrant parent)	137.94 (146.96)	145.17 (151.48)	154.80
Immigrants from Western countries	153.31 (163.33)	157.81 (164.67)	168.48
Immigrants from non-Western countries	129.73 (138.21)	134.94 (140.80)	138.00
Total	138.16 (147.14)	145.28 (151.59)	154.69

Note: Western countries are EU countries, Norway, Switzerland, Iceland, North America, Australia and New Zealand; non-Western countries are all other countries. Those aged 18-65 years with a positive hourly wage less than 10,000 kroner are included. Those with income as self-employed are excluded.

FIGURE 5.3.

The structure of hourly wage rate among immigrants from non-Western countries in 1998 (in Danish *kroner*)

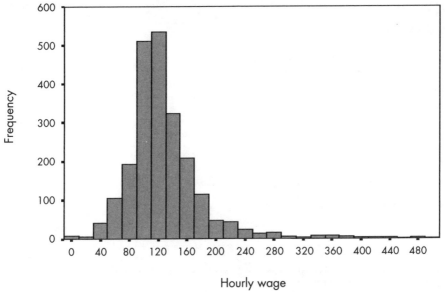

Note: Number of observations: 2,233, average hourly wage: 127.96, standard deviation 54.98. Only those aged 18-65 with an hourly wage larger than zero and equal to or less than 500 kroner are included (around 1 per cent have an hourly wage of 500 kroner or more). Those with income as self-employed are excluded.

In Table 5.5 the average hourly wage rates for 1995, 1996 and 1998 are presented. Note that the real wage rate for immigrants from non-Western countries is lower in 1998 than in 1996. This is probably explained by the higher employment rate for this group in 1998 and that many of those who are newly hired are in relatively low-paid jobs.

5.2 The demographic structure

Redistribution via the public sector is very much redistribution between generations – from those of active age to children and old people. If the groups differ much from each other in age structure the consequences could be important. We shall therefore give a short description of the age structure for the different groups. In Table 5.6 the average age is shown for the groups of active age in 1995, 1996, 1997 and 1998. The group that differs most from the others is the second-generation immigrant group. They are younger, especially those from non-Western countries. The main reason for

TABLE 5.6.

Average age for those aged 18 years or older

GROUP	1995	1996	1997	1998
Danish population (excluding those who have one immigrant parent)	46.9	47.1	47.2	47.4
Second generation – one Danish parent and one immigrant parent from a Western country	28.2	28.4	29.0	29.4
Second generation – one Danish parent and one immigrant parent from a non-Western country	26.5	26.2	26.9	27.4
Immigrants from Western countries	48.3	47.8	47.5	47.5
Second generation – parents from Western countries	39.9	40.3	40.6	40.6
Immigrants from non-Western countries	36.9	38.1	38.4	37.6
Second generation – parents from non-Western countries	23.1	23.0	22.7	22.7
Total	46.3	46.5	46.6	46.7

Note: Western countries are EU countries, Norway, Switzerland, Iceland, North America, Australia and New Zealand; non-Western countries are all other countries.

this is that immigration from these countries has mainly been a phenomenon of the last decades and it means that few of these immigrants' children, who were born in Denmark, have reached active age, and that those who are of active age are young. It should be stressed here that few children of immigrants who were born before 1960 are registered as second-generation immigrants due to a lack of information in the registers. This means that the majority of the older second-generation immigrants are not counted as belonging to that group which of course reduced the average age as seen in the statistics. Another problem is that most of the immigrants and second-generation immigrants who have received Danish citizenship before 1978 are included in the Danish population.

From the table we can see that the average age increased somewhat between 1995 and 1998. It is especially so for those groups who have one parent who was born abroad and one parent who was born in Denmark. The average age is however a blunt measure of the age structure. Here we shall present some more information by giving the age structure for broad age categories. There are two different classifications. In the first, children 17 years or younger are classified according to which group their parents belong. In the second one, children are classified according to their own group. This makes a great difference as most children of immigrants were born in Denmark and are classified as first generation immigrants in the first clas-

TABLE 5.7.

Age structure in 1998 for the different groups. Children 17 years and younger classified according to the status of their parents. Percentage distribution

GROUP	0-17	18-24	25-34	35-54	55-64	65-
Danish population (excluding those who have one immigrant parent)	20.1	8.7	14.6	29.5	11.4	15.7
Second generation – one Danish parent and one immigrant parent from a Western country	14.5	26.4	36.2	22.9	0	0
Second generation – one Danish parent and one immigrant parent from a non-Western country	18.6	36.3	29.3	15.8	0	0
Immigrants from Western countries	19.2	6.2	15.7	32.8	11.9	14.2
Second generation – parents from Western countries	24.5	11.5	19.4	31.8	4.8	8.0
Immigrants from non-Western countries	35.8	9.7	21.7	25.4	4.4	3.0
Second generation – parents from non-Western countries	11.7	67.3	16.2	4.5	0	0.3
Total	20.9	9.0	15.3	29.2	10.9	14.7

Note: Western countries are EU countries, Norway, Switzerland, Iceland, North America, Australia and New Zealand; non-Western countries are all other countries.

sification scheme and as second-generation immigrants in the second scheme. See Table 5.7 and 5.8.

The share in active age (18-64 years) is higher among immigrants (78.1 per cent of immigrants from Western countries and 80.6 for those from non-Western countries) than among the Danish population (64.2 per cent), if children 17 years and younger are classified according to their own status (Table 5.8). The age structure for immigrants differs considerably from that for the Danish population. The immigrants from non-Western countries are under-represented among the older people, and the immigrants from Western countries among young people, if measured by the classification method used in Table 5.8. Measured by that method, all four groups of second-generation immigrants are highly over-represented among those who are 17 years of age or younger.

Men and women have different positions in the labour market and also different roles in the family. It is also so that after divorce, children continue to live with their

TABLE 5.8.

Age structure in 1998 for the different groups. Children 17 years and younger classified according to the status of their own. Percentage distribution

GROUP	0-17	18-24	25-34	35-54	55-64	65-
Danish population (excluding those who have one immigrant parent)	20.1	8.7	14.6	29.4	11.5	15.7
Second generation – one Danish parent and one immigrant parent from a Western country	41.8	18.0	24.6	15.6	0	0
Second generation – one Danish parent and one immigrant parent from a non-Western country	66.0	15.1	12.2	6.7	0	0
Immigrants from Western countries	5.3	7.2	18.4	38.6	13.9	16.6
Second generation – parents from Western countries	34.9	9.9	16.8	27.4	4.1	6.9
Immigrants from non-Western countries	15.4	12.8	28.5	33.5	5.8	4.0
Second generation – parents from non-Western countries	86.8	10.0	2.4	0.7	0	0.1
Total	21.1	9.0	15.2	29.1	10.9	14.7

Note: Western countries are EU countries, Norway, Switzerland, Iceland, North America, Australia and New Zealand; non-Western countries are all other countries.

mothers to a much higher extent than with their fathers and therefore the mothers receive the support that is directed to the children. In the calculation where the net transfer to the child is counted as part of the parents' net transfer this is of great importance. It means that the relative numbers of men and women in a group may be important for the calculated net transfer. Table 5.9 shows the gender composition is more or less the same in the various groups.

5.3 The development of the net transfers in the 1990s

We shall now study how the net transfers have changed between 1991 and 1998. Table 5.10 shows the size of the net transfers for the various groups per individual. The net transfers are positive for the total population (to public consumption and investments not distributed on individuals) and increase between 1991 and 1998. The increase is especially large between 1996 and 1997.

TABLE 5.9.
Percentage of men among those 18 years or older

GROUP	1995	1996	1997	1998
Danish population (excluding those who have one immigrant parent)	48.9	48.7	48.9	48.9
Second generation – one Danish parent and one immigrant parent from a Western country	53.2	51.3	50.9	53.3
Second generation – one Danish parent and one immigrant parent from a non-Western country	48.9	56.4	55.8	48.4
Immigrants from Western countries	46.1	45.5	45.1	47.6
Second generation – parents from Western countries	55.8	51.2	51.4	55.3
Immigrants from non-Western countries	47.9	50.6	49.8	50.5
Second generation – parents from non-Western countries	53.3	50.5	52.6	49.5
Total	49.0	48.8	48.9	49.0

Note: Western countries are EU countries, Norway, Switzerland, Iceland, North America, Australia and New Zealand; non-Western countries are all other countries.

Of special interest is the size of the net transfers to immigrants and how they change over time. For immigrants from Western countries, in all five years covered by this study, there is a net transfer *to* the public sector from the immigrants. The net transfer declined between 1991 and 1995 but has increased since then and was considerably higher in 1998 than in 1991.

For immigrants from non-Western countries there is a net transfer in all years in the other direction, from the public sector to the immigrants. The net transfer to the immigrants was considerably larger in 1995 and 1996 than in 1991, but in 1997 was back to a level somewhere between the level in 1995 and 1991 if calculated at constant prices. The change between 1996 and 1997 was large, 9 per cent, and the change between 1997 and 1998 was even larger, 13 per cent. The level is now the same as in 1991. The development follows the development in the labour market situation. As shown earlier in this chapter, unemployment has declined and the labour force participation has increased among non-Western immigrants in the last few years.

TABLE 5.10.

Net transfers to the public sector (in Danish *kroner*) per person for different groups in 1991, 1995, 1996, 1997 and 1998. (Amounts in 1997 prices in parentheses)

GROUP	1991	1995	1996	1997	1998
Danish population (excluding those who have one immigrant parent)	13,600 (14,900)	15,800 (16,500)	18,600 (19,000)	22,700	25,000 (24,500)
Danish population (including those who have one immigrant parent)	13,600 (14,900)	15,900 (16,600)	18,700 (19,100)	22,800	25,100 (24,600)
Second generation – one Danish parent and one immigrant parent from a Western country	17,700 (19,500)	25,700 (26,500)	29,600 (30,200)	31,000	33,100 (32,500)
Second generation – one Danish parent and one immigrant parent from a non-Western country	4,900 (5,400)	14,500 (15,100)	12,400 (12,700)	19,000	27,800 (27,300)
Second generation – two parents from Western countries	19,600 (21,500)	18,900 (19,700)	27,500 (28,100)	34,400	19,600 (19,200)
Immigrants from Western countries	14,500 (15,900)	9,400 (9,800)	10,900 (11,100)	13,000	23,900 (23,500)
Immigrants from Western countries (first and second generation)	14,900 (16,400)	10,700 (11,100)	12,300 (12,600)	14,700	23,500 (23,100)
Second generation – two parents from non-Western countries	700 (800)	-32,300 (-33,700)	-11,600 (-11,800)	-13,100	2,000 (2,000)
Immigrants from non-Western countries	-48,900 (-53,700)	-63,900 (-66,600)	-66,000 (-67,400)	-60,300	-54,000 (-53,000)
Immigrants from non-Western countries (first and second generation)	-48,000 (-52,800)	-62,600 (-65,300)	-63,700 (-65,000)	-58,200	-51,500 (-50,500)
Total	12,000 (13200)	12,600 (13,100)	15,000 (15,300)	19,500	21,900 (21,500)

Note: Western countries are EU countries, Norway, Switzerland, Iceland, North America, Australia and New Zealand; non-Western countries are all other countries.

If we compare the Danish group and the non-Western group (including second generation immigrants) we find a difference of 76,500 *kroner* in 1998. Of the difference more than half, 44,000 *kroner*, can be traced to taxes, 17,500 to public transfers and 15,000 to other public expenditure. Most of the differences in tax payments are due to differences in personal taxes (mainly the income tax) and can be explained by the immigrants having lower earnings. As regards transfers, the immigrants receive less in pensions and early pensions (*efterløn*), but more in the form of support at unemployment and social welfare including support to cover dwelling costs. The differences depend on differences in age structure, the number of children and the employment situation. As regards public consumption, Danes get more in the form of old age care and the immigrants more for childcare and education – differences, which can be explained by differences in age structure.

The results shown here are not specific for Denmark. According to a study for Norway in 1993 the net transfer *from* the public sector to refugees was 62,000 Norwegian *kroner* per person. The corresponding net transfer from Norwegians *to* the public sector was 2,400 Norwegian *kroner* per person; and from immigrants other than refugees, 1,500 per person *to* the public sector.[66]

A question lively discussed in the U.S. is whether the economic situation of immigrants is improved by the period of residence in the country of immigration and if the net transfers also gradually decline as a result.[67] Table 5.11 contains information on net transfers in relation to the length of time immigrants from non-Western countries have been in Denmark. It shows that the net transfers are lower for those who have been in Denmark for a longer period than for those who have been in the country for a shorter time. There is one exception: net transfers to those who were less than a year in Denmark[68] and, in 1998, also those who had arrived 1–3 years earlier. However, for lengths of stay of up to ten years, the differences are rather small and for those with ten years of stay or more the amount is smaller but it is still quite high. If we compare groups with the same length of stay in the five years covered, we will in most cases find the same development as for all non-Western immigrants.

The type of comparisons presented here should be interpreted with care. They cannot be interpreted as indicating the degree of integration for new immigrants over time. Things other than assimilation may explain differences between immigrants who have lived in Denmark for different lengths of time. First, the composition of immigrants arriving in the country may differ in different years. Second, the return migration may be selective.

---

66 See ECON (1996) and Larsen & Bruse (1998). Note that in the Norwegian calculations they refer to the net transfer per person of all age groups, not as in the calculations for Denmark which are distributed only on those 18 years and older. If the same method had been used for the Danish data the values would have been lower than those shown here.

67 See for example Chiswick (1978) and Borjas (1994, 1998).

68 It can be explained by the fact that many in this group had been in Denmark for only part of the year and therefore the public expenditure is of course less than if they had resided in the country the whole year.

TABLE 5.11.

Net transfers to the public sector (in Danish *kroner*) per person from non-Western countries according to length of stay in Denmark in 1991, 1995, 1996, 1997 and 1998. (Amounts in 1997 prices in parentheses)

LENGTH OF STAY*	1991	1995	1996	1997	1998
Less than one year	-45,200 (-49,700)	-82,000 (-85,400)	-55,800 (-57,000)	-45,500	-25,800 (-25,300)
1-3 years	-63,200 (-69,500)	-56,600 (-58,400)	-89,900 (-91,800)	-79,900	-49,800 (-48,900)
3-5 years	-65,400 (-71,900)	-76,300 (-79,400)	-79,300 (-81,000)	-78,300	-76,000 (-74,600)
5-7 years	-70,300 (-77,300)	-79,300 (-82,600)	-83,600 (-85,400)	-71,500	-74,400 (-73,000)
7-10 years	-40,400 (-44,400)	-76,600 (-79,800)	-82,100 (-83,800)	-70,500	-75,100 (-73,700)
10 years or more	-34,100 (-37,500)	-49,000 (-51,100)	-46,700 (-47,700)	-46,000	-42,100 (-41,300)
Second generation	700 (800)	-32,300 (-33,700)	-11,600 (-11,800)	-13,100	2,000 (2,000)
Total	-48,000 (-52,800)	-62,600 (-65,300)	-63,700 (-65,000)	-58,200	-51,500 (-50,500)

*The division according to length of stay is based on exact age. 'Less than one year' in the column for the year 1996 includes those who immigrated on 1 January 1996 or later, '1-3 years' includes those who immigrated between 1 January 1994 and 31 December 1995, etc.

Up to now we have shown the net transfer to the public sector per person. There are good arguments also to present the total net transfer from or to immigrants. The size of total net transfers depends not only on the average value but also on the number of immigrants. It is the total net transfers that have been the focus of the political debate. To make it possible to compare values for the different years, we have presented actual figures for each year as well as their relevant values in 1997. To make it easier to get a feeling for the size of the total net transfer, it is also related to the size of the GDP.[69]

Table 5.12 shows that the total net transfer in constant prices and also as part of GDP increased greatly between 1991 and 1995 and continued to increase in 1996. It

69   Only those who have been resident in Denmark at the end of the year are included in the figures. Those who have been resident in Denmark only part of the year but not in the end of the year are not included (emigrants and deceased). As the return migration is high it could be a problem, but as far as we can see the exclusion of those groups is only a minor problem.

TABLE 5.12.

Total net transfers to the public sector (in million Danish *kroner*) for different groups in 1991, 1995, 1996, 1997 and 1998. (Amounts in 1997 prices are in parentheses)

	GROUP	1991	1995	1996	1997	1998
(1)	Second generation – parents from Western countries	124 (136)	123 (128)	205 (209)	253	139 (136)
(2)	Immigrants from Western countries	1,046 (1,150)	808 (842)	912 (931)	1,051	2,105 (2,066)
(3) = (1)+(2)	Immigrants from Western countries (first and second generation)	1,170 (1,285)	931 (970)	1,117 (1,140)	1,304	2,244 (2,202)
(4)	Second generation – parents from non-Western countries	1 (1)	-147 (-153)	-69 (-70)	-92	16 (16)
(5)	Immigrants from non-Western countries	-4,855 (-5,336)	-8421 (-8,775)	-9,672 (-9,875)	-9,220	-8,793 (-8,629)
(6)= (4)+(5)	Immigrants from non-Western countries (first and second generation)	-4,854 (-5,335)	-8,568 (-8,928)	-9,741 (-9,946)	-9,312	-8,777 (-8,613)
(7) = (3)+(6)	All immigrants (first and second generation)	-3,684 (-4,049)	-7,637 (-7,958)	-8,624 (-8,805)	-8,008	-6,533 (-6,411)
(8)	Immigrants from Western countries (first and second generation) as per cent of GDP	+0.13	+0.09	+0.10	+0.12	+0.19
(9)	Immigrants from non-Western countries (first and second generation) as per cent of GDP	-0.54	-0.85	-0.91	-0.84	-0.75
(10) = (8)+(9)	All immigrants (7) as per cent of GDP	-0.41	-0.76	-0.81	-0.72	-0.56

Note: Western countries are EU countries, Norway, Switzerland, Iceland, North America, Australia and New Zealand; non-Western countries are all other countries.

is mainly explained by increases in the number of immigrants from non-Western countries. The net transfer to each immigrant declined between 1995 and 1996 but the number of immigrants increased so much that the total net transfers to the immigrants became larger, as did the transfers as a share of GDP. Between 1996 and 1997 the total net transfers declined by 7 per cent and between 1997 and 1998 by 7.5 per cent. The net transfers per person declined more than the number of immigrants expanded. As a share of the GDP the net transfers were considerably smaller in 1998 than in 1995 but considerably larger than in 1991.

Dividing the immigrants according to countries of origin, we see that the net transfer from the Western immigrants to the public sector fell from 1991 to 1995 and later gradually increased. For immigrants from non-Western countries the transfers from the public sector increased greatly between 1991 and 1995 from 0.54 to 0.85 per cent of the GDP. The share continued to increase in 1996 but declined in 1997 to a level below that of 1995, and in 1998 to a level much lower than that in 1995.

These figures can be compared with those for Sweden. A study by Jan Ekberg (1999) shows that the net transfers to immigrants in Sweden were 0.9 per cent in 1991 and 2.0 per cent in 1994 as a share of the GDP. The numbers are twice those of Denmark but the immigrant population is also twice as high in Sweden as in Denmark measured as a per cent of the population. The large increase between 1991 and 1994 can partly be explained by large immigration during those years, but also – and mainly – by the drastically worsening labour market situation. For Norway we have a calculation for 1993 showing that the total net transfers to immigrants was 3.6 billion (see ECON, 1996). Compared to the GDP the same year this is 0.44 per cent, a higher value than that for Denmark in 1991 but lower than that for Denmark in 1995.

5.4 Conclusions

In this chapter we have examined the employment situation and the demographic composition of Danes and immigrants and also the development of net transfers during the time period 1991-1998 using aggregate data. Compared to Danes and Western immigrants, the non-Western immigrants have a low employment rate (share of the group's population that is employed). The labour force participation rate is lower and the unemployment rate higher among those in the labour force.

The low employment rate is one part of the explanation for the negative net transfers from non-Western immigrants; another part of the explanation is that on average they have lower hourly wages. A lower employment rate and a lower wage rate means less tax paid and more transfers received, and while the employment rate has increased during the time period studied, the difference compared to the Danes is still large.

Examining the net transfers per person, it can be seen that on average from 1991 to 1998 net transfers to the public sector increased from all groups, most likely as a result of the improved labour market situation. Nevertheless, net transfers from the public sector to non-Western immigrants increased in total until 1996. This can be explained by the fact that even though the average net transfer to immigrants declined between 1995 and 1996, the number of immigrants increased more. From 1997 the total net transfers to the non-Western immigrants have declined.

In the next chapters, by using individual data we will analyse in more detail the factors behind the structure of redistribution through the public sector.

Chapter 6

Factors Influencing Net Transfer
to the Public Sector: A Study Based
on Cross-Sectional Data

In order to examine the pattern of redistribution in more detail we have to use individual data. In this chapter individual information from 1996, 1997 and 1998 is used to analyse how factors such as age, length of stay, family composition and the individual employment rate influence the net transfers. In this chapter we use data in which the net transfers to children 17 years or younger are added to that of their parents.

In the first section regression estimations are presented for 1998, the latest year covered by this study. The estimates point to large effects of family status and the employment rate on the net transfer. In the second section net transfers in 1996, 1997 and 1998 are compared, by including variables representing 1997 and 1998 in a merged sample. In the third section, differences between the employment rates of various groups are studied, and whether there are any differences in effects of the employment rate on net transfers between the groups. In the fourth section the net transfer rate according to age is shown for all, independent of the employment rate, for those with an employment rate of 100 and for those with an employment rate of 0. In all three cases, results are shown separately for the Danish group, Western immigrants and non-Western immigrants.

6.1 The pattern of net transfer in 1998

To study the pattern of net transfer in more detail, regression analysis will be used. Table 6.1 contains four regression estimations using data from 1998 where new groups of variables are added stepwise. In equation (1) only the variables representing immigrant status are included, in equation (2) the demographic variables (gender, age, and family status) are added, while in equation (3) the employment rate is also included. In equation (4), earnings replace the employment rate.

We find that only about 1 per cent of the variation in net transfers is explained by the variables representing immigrant status. This is because immigrants constitute such a small part of the sample, i.e., the greater part of the variation in the net transfers is a variation within the Danish group. When the demographic variables of gender, age, and family status are added, 22 per cent of the variation in net transfers is

TABLE 6.1.

Regression estimates (OLS) with net transfer to the public sector in 1998 (in thousand Danish *kroner*) as the dependent variable; and age, gender, family status, country of origin, employment rate and earnings as independent variables

VARIABLES	(1)	(2)	(3)	(4)
Constant	22.911 (0.411)	-139.971 (2.514)	-173.899 (2.071)	-126.236 (1.844)
Born in Denmark				
Both parents born in Denmark	0	0	0	0
One parent born in Denmark, one in a Western country	9.320 (3.800)	-1.259 (3.395)	8.985 (2.279)	0.207 (2.490)
One parent born in Denmark, one in a non-Western country	3.130 (7.497)	-0.104 (6.669)	17.765 (5.483)	-1.029 (4.892)
Both parents born in a Western country	-3.570 (9.673)	-13.446 (8.584)	10.502 (7.058)	-1.635 (6.297)
Both parents born in a non-Western country	-23.658 (9.014)	-8.438 (8.028)	27.562 (6.601)	20.623 (5.889)
Born outside Denmark				
Born in Western country	0.917 (2.776)	-1.625 (2.463)	25.093 (2.028)	11.608 (1.807)
Born in non-Western country	-77.417 (2.065)	-90.298 (1.848)	-12.708 (1.548)	-17.910 (1.371)
Female		-56.610 (0.716)	-33.420 (0.595)	-20.517 (0.535)
Age		10.648 (0.113)	4.851 (0.095)	3.952 (0.085)
Age^2		-0.126 (0.001)	-0.048 (0.001)	-0.054 (0.001)
Family status				
Unmarried, no children		0	0	0
Unmarried with children		-88.525 (2.272)	-98.621 (1.865)	-101.202 (1.667)
Married, no children		33.796 (1.094)	15.682 (0.738)	20.308 (0.657)
Married with children		0.244 (1.012)	-42.062 (0.848)	-43.455 (0.753)
Employment rate			2.058 (0.008)	
Earnings				0.700 (0.002)
N	139,701	139,701	139,701	139,701
R^2(adj)	0.010	0.221	0.473	0.581

Note. Standard errors in parentheses. Only persons 18 years and older are included. Married stands for living together, irrespective of whether a couple is formally married or not.

explained, while 47 per cent is explained when the employment rate is also added. Substituting the employment rate with earnings leads to an even higher rate of explanation, 58 per cent. The earnings capture both the effect of the employment and the effect of the individual's hourly wage rate.

According to the first equation there are two immigrant groups that have significantly less positive transfers to the public sector than the Danish group. In one of these cases, non-Western immigrants, the estimations show that the group is a net transfer receiver. Immigrants who were born in Western countries have a positive transfer to the public sector of about the same size as that for the Danish group. One group, those who have one parent who was born in Denmark and one born in a Western country, has a significantly larger net transfer to the public sector than the Danish group.

When we add the demographic variables – age, gender, and family status[70] – the effects remain for the non-Western immigrants with an even larger size of the coefficient. Hence, the fact that immigrants from non-Western countries receive more from the public sector cannot be explained by differences in the composition of age, gender, and family status. Instead, the age composition of this group makes us expect redistribution *from* the group. The net transfers from the individuals with one Danish parent and one parent from a Western country and for those with both parents born in a non-Western country are no longer significantly different from that of the Danish group when the demographic variables are included in the estimations.

When we also include the employment rate, the coefficients for the immigrant groups change dramatically. For four groups – the two groups with one Danish and one immigrant parent, the group with both parents born in a non-Western country and the immigrants born in Western countries – the coefficients turn significantly positive. It means that the net transfer from the groups to the public sector is larger than the one from Danes with the same age, gender, family status, and employment rate. For non-Western immigrants the value of the coefficient is considerably smaller when the employment rate is included, but it is still significantly negative.

---

70 Estimations with a more detailed division of the family status have been performed. The division has been made according to gender and marital status, and in addition according to the number of children (0, 1, 2, 3, 4 or more). The adjusted R^2 value increases to 0.247 in the equation corresponding to equation (2), to 0.489 in the equation corresponding to equation (3) and to 0.592 in the equation corresponding to equation (4). The estimated coefficients for the other variables do not change much. The coefficient representing non-Western countries changes from –12.708 to –8.458; that is, a part of the effect is eliminated.

When earnings replace the employment rate, several of the coefficients for the immigrant groups turn insignificant. However, those whose parents were born in non-Western countries and persons born in a Western country still have net transfers that are significantly larger than the Danes, and the coefficient for immigrants from non-Western countries is still negative (and even larger in this case than in the former case).

When it comes to the other variables the signs are as expected. An equation of the second degree gives a good fit for the age variable, indicating that the transfers take place from those of active age to those of passive age (younger and older individuals).[71] Differences between family status also imply that there is a transfer between generations and, as expected, the transfers go to those who have children.[72] The coefficient for net transfer to those who are unmarried with children is twice as high as that for those who are married with children. The explanation for this is that the net transfers to children are split in two for a married couple but not for a single parent. There is also an important difference between men and women; the net transfers are substantially larger to women, even if the effect decreases when controlling for employment or earnings.[73] A part of the difference is explained by the subsidy to children that is generally paid to the woman and also is assigned to the woman when the parents are married, though it also can be seen as a contribution to the family or to the child.

The value of the coefficient for the employment rate indicates that a change of employment rate for one person from 0 to 100 means an effect on the net transfer to the public sector of about 200,000 Danish *kroner*.

The value of the coefficient for the earnings variable, 0.700, shows a marginal effect of 70 per cent. An increase in the earnings of 1,000 Danish *kroner* leads to an increase in the net transfer to the public sector of 700 Danish *kroner*. The estimates indicate the influence of the two most important ways of redistribution through the public sector – over the life cycle and between the employed and the unemployed.

Estimations of the same kind as those presented here, but with variables representing the length of stay included, are shown in Appendix Table 6.A1. As can be

---

71   We have also done estimations with dummy variables representing age in five-year intervals. The adjusted R^2 value becomes about the same. In order to present the tables in a less comprehensive form, only the alternative with age in a linear and a quadratic form is shown.

72   As previously mentioned the transfers to children who are under 18 years old are assigned to the parents.

73   See Fritzell (1998) for an analysis concerning the redistribution between men and women that takes place through public services.

TABLE 6.2.

Regression estimates (OLS) with net transfer to the public sector in 1998 (in thousand Danish *kroner*) as the dependent variable; and age, gender, family status, country of origin, employment rate, hourly wages and earnings as independent variables for those who have a positive wage rate and who are not self-employed

VARIABLES	(1)	(2)	(3)
Constant	-152.601	-160.331	-46.200
	(3.458)	(3.384)	(2.194)
Born in Denmark			
Both parents born in Denmark	0	0	0
One parent born in Denmark, one in a Western country	7.272	6.797	-1.352
	(2.528)	(2.472)	(1.588)
One parent born in Denmark, one in a non-Western country	18.469	17.267	-3.750
	(4.896)	(4.788)	(3.076)
Both parents born in a Western country	12.263	8.549	1.413
	(7.370)	(7.208)	(4.631)
Both parents born in a non-Western country	4.775	5.889	-3.738
	(6.430)	(6.288)	(4.040)
Born outside Denmark			
Born in Western country	13.108	13.271	6.620
	(2.347)	(2.295)	(1.474)
Born in non-Western country	-20.732	-19.739	-0.439
	(1.921)	(1.879)	(1.207)
Female	-40.278	-37.438	-3.087
	(0.631)	(0.619)	(0.410)
Age	4.422	3.957	-1.373
	(0.204)	(0.200)	(0.127)
Age^2	-0.037	-0.033	0.019
	(0.003)	(0.002)	(0.002)
Family status			
Unmarried, no children	0	0	0
Unmarried with children	-98.347	-98.335	-101.588
	(1.877)	(1.836)	(1.180)
Married, no children	3.390	2.918	-1.469
	(0.851)	(0.832)	(0.534)
Married with children	-46.493	-47.578	-58.191
	(0.888)	(0.869)	(0.559)
Employment rate	1.870	1.947	
	(0.012)	(0.011)	
Hourly wages		0.007	
		(0.001)	
Earnings			0.790
			(0.002)
N	78,180	78,180	78,180
R^2(adj)	0.410	0.436	0.767

Note. Standard errors in parentheses. Only persons 18 years and older with positive hourly wages are included. Married stands for living together, irrespective of whether a couple is formally married or not.

seen from the table there are some differences between individuals from non-Western countries with different lengths of stay. The pattern is difficult to interpret however. When considering the equation where the demographic variables are included, but not the employment rate we cannot find a clear pattern that can be reasonably interpreted. One exception is that the transfers are lower to those who have lived in Denmark for more than 12 years than for those who have been in Denmark for a shorter period. This is also valid when a more detailed division by family type with respect to the number of children is done.

In Table 6.2 the results from further estimations are presented. Here the sample is reduced to those who have an hourly wage rate that is greater than zero, i.e. they have been employed during the year and who have not been self-employed.[74] The first equation is estimated with immigrant status, the demographic variables and the employment rate, and consequently consists of the same variables as equation (3) in Table 6.1. The coefficients turn out to be rather similar to the corresponding equation in Table 6.1, with exceptions for the coefficients for females and for the variable indicating birth in a non-Western country, which have become more negative and for the variables for both parents born in a non-Western country and birth in a Western country, which have become less positive. Equation (2) in Table 6.2 includes hourly wages as an explanatory variable, which reduces the impact of the variables for females and birth in a non-Western country, but increases the impact of employment rate. In equation (3), earnings replace the employment rate and the hourly wages. It increases the share of variation explained. It indicates that the transfers and the taxes are determined not mainly by the employment rate or the wage rate but by the earnings. The value of the coefficient is 0.790. The implicit marginal effect is slightly higher in this case than in the case when all persons age 18 or over were included.

---

74 For a more detailed description of how the hourly wages are calculated, see Chapter 5.

TABLE 6.3.

Regression estimates (OLS) with net transfer to the public sector (in thousand Danish *kroner* in 1997 prices) in 1996, 1997 and 1998 as the dependent variable; and age, gender, family status, country of origin, and employment rate as independent variables

VARIABLES	(1)	(2)	(3)
Constant	18.168 (0.398)	-136.268 (1.461)	-167.161 (1.209)
1997 sample	4.005 (0.556)	3.488 (0.497)	2.046 (0.410)
1998 sample	4.674 (0.555)	3.909 (0.497)	0.141 (0.410)
Born in Denmark			
Both parents born in Denmark	0	0	0
One parent born in Denmark, one in a Western country	9.206 (2.199)	0.324 (1.976)	10.926 (1.633)
One parent born in Denmark, one in a non-Western country	-2.964 (4.488)	-5.475 (4.017)	16.483 (3.318)
Both parents born in a Western country	5.829 (5.429)	-0.793 (4.848)	12.019 (4.004)
Both parents born in a non-Western country	-32.332 (5.455)	-18.354 (4.885)	15.373 (4.036)
Born outside Denmark			
Born in Western country	-5.115 (1.613)	-6.468 (1.441)	19.049 (1.192)
Born in non-Western country	-81.464 (1.205)	-92.769 (1.083)	-14.194 (0.913)
Female		-55.392 (0.441)	-32.035 (0.343)
Age		10.181 (0.064)	4.578 (0.055)
Age^2		-0.120 (0.001)	-0.045 (0.001)
Family status			
Unmarried, no children		0	0
Unmarried with children		-87.423 (1.288)	-95.784 (1.064)
Married, no children		32.447 (0.513)	15.058 (0.426)
Married with children		0.526 (0.580)	-40.099 (0.488)
Employment rate			2.008 (0.005)
N	417,376	417,376	417,376
R^2(adj)	0.011	0.212	0.462

Note. Standard errors in parentheses. Only those who are 18 years or older are included. Married stands for living together, irrespective of whether a couple is formally married or not.

6.2 Changes in net transfer between 1996 and 1998

We have individual cross sectional data of the same type for three years, 1996, 1997 and 1998. This enables us to look at some parts of the analysis in more depth and we will use two possibilities. First, we will see whether having more observations when combining data from three years leads to a greater exactness in the estimations. Second, we will study the changes between 1996 and 1998.

Table 6.3 corresponds to Table 6.1 in all respects but two. Observations from 1996, 1997 and 1998 are included and there are two variables indicating that the observation stems from either 1997 or 1998 and hence a comparison to 1996 can be made.[75] To make the net transfers for different years comparable, the values for 1996 and 1998 have been recalculated in 1997 prices.

We will first examine the dummy variables representing the year 1997 and the year 1998, respectively. The first equation, where variables indicating country of origin for the individual and his/her parents are included, implies an increase in the net transfer of 4,000 *kroner* between 1996 and 1997. This amount is reduced to 3,500 when the demographic variables are also included, as can be seen from equation (2). If we also add the employment rate the amount decreases to 2,000 *kroner*, see equation (3). This can be interpreted in that the increased employment rate explains the increase in the net transfers to the public sector with 1,500 *kroner* between 1996 and 1997 (3,500-2,000), and the 500 *kroner* is explained by a change in the demographic composition (4,000-3,500). The rest, 2,000 *kroner* is explained by something else, for example economic growth or changes in the redistribution system (taxes, transfers) and public consumption (health care, education etc.). When comparing 1996 and 1998 the corresponding figures become 3,800, 800, and 100. If we consider the change between 1997 and 1998 the figures turn out to be 2,400, 200 and –1,900.

If we could measure the employment rate and the demographic composition in a more precise way, perhaps more could be explained by changes in these variables. When we add variables representing length of the stay in Denmark (see Appendix Table 6.A2), the values of the variables representing the years 1997 and 1998 do not change much. The size and the effects are about the same.

The next step is to see how the coefficients and their standard errors change when we have more observations. The results from such a comparison can be concluded in the following way. The estimated coefficients do not change to any great extent. However, as expected the standard errors decrease, particularly for the smaller immi-

---

75   It has not been possible to re-estimate equation (4) in Table 6.1 since we do not have information on earnings for 1996 and 1997.

FIGURE 6.1.

Employment rate (three-year average) in per cent in 1998 among Danes, Western immigrants, and non-Western immigrants. Women

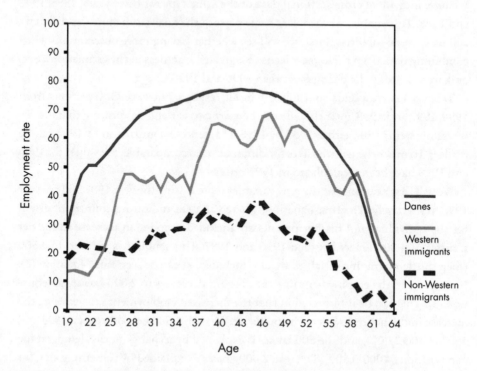

grant groups. In some cases we get a significant difference compared to the Danish group, even when this difference was not significant in the smaller sample. This indicates the importance of further increasing the sample.

6.3 The employment rate

As previously shown, differences in the employment rate between the groups are very large.[76] With some figures we will now show the extent of these differences. Although the number of observations is smaller for the two groups of immigrants, which leads to larger variations in the curves, the main patterns for the three groups are easy to see.

Figure 6.1 shows substantial differences in the employment rate between Danish women and immigrant women. Between Danish women and women from Western

---

76 These differences in employment can be found in most countries that receive immigrants. A
    similar pattern of employment for New Zealand is found in Winkelmann (1999).

FIGURE 6.2.

Employment rate (three-year average) in per cent in 1998 among Danes, Western immigrants, and non-Western immigrants. Men

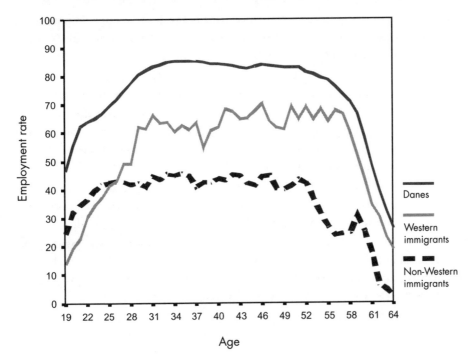

countries there is a clear difference until 58 years of age. The difference is greatest for the younger women and a possible explanation could be that a higher percentage of Western immigrants are full-time students (some may be guest students).[77] Among those over the age of 50 the employment rate is about the same. Women from non-Western countries have a very low employment rate irrespective of age, and for those over 60 it is extremely low. A possible explanation might be that some of the women in this latter age group – having retired in their home country – had recently come to join relatives living in Denmark. Of the women between 60-64 years old from these countries in 1998, 45 per cent had arrived in 1986 or later, and as many as 34

---

77   There are no satisfactory statistics covering the number of guest students. However, Frederik Hansen has estimated the number of guest students by means of register data (Ministry of Economic Affairs, 25 June 1999, Definition af 'Gæststuderende'). Categorised as guest students are those who started to study upon arriving in Denmark (or shortly afterwards). The total number of guest students was 1,600 in 1997. The greater part, about 90 per cent, came from Western countries.

per cent during 1995-1998. The corresponding figures for women from Western countries in the same ages are 9 and 5 per cent, respectively.

Figure 6.2 shows that the pattern is the same for men as for women. There are considerable differences in the employment rate between the groups. In particular, the average employment rate for non-Western immigrants is substantially lower than the employment rate for Danes, but it is also lower than the employment rate for Western immigrants. As for the women, the low rates of employment among non-Western immigrants aged 60-64 years should not be interpreted as though the younger cohorts will also experience this low employment rate when they reach the same ages. 40 per cent of men from non-Western countries, 60-64 years old, arrived in 1986 or later and 25 per cent in 1995-1998. The corresponding figures for Western immigrants are 25 and 15 per cent.

Another way of showing the importance of the employment rate is to use the estimated coefficients. First, we will use equation (3) in Table 6.1. First, we insert in the equation the average values for the variables age, age^2, gender, and family status for the non-Western immigrant group and value 1 for the variable representing the non-Western immigrant group. The net transfer then becomes –105,200 *kroner* when the employment rate is zero, 100,600 *kroner* when the employment rate is 100 per cent, and -42,200 at the actual employment rate (30.6 per cent). The employment rate that makes the net transfer equal to zero is 51.1 per cent. This means that the employment rate needs to increase by 20.5 percentage points (51.1-30.6), to make the net transfer turn zero.[78]

Secondly, we use the estimates from equation 3 in Table 6.1 to predict the net transfer in 1999 (a year for which we do not yet have information). As the unemployment rate declined and the labour force increased between 1998 and 1999 we can expect that the net transfer will be reduced from 1998 to 1999. We use equation (3) in Table 6.1 and assume that the relation will be the same, that other variables will not change, and that the employment rate will change in the same way as indicated by Table 5.1 and 5.2. The net transfer to a non-Western immigrant will be reduced by 4,000 *kroner* between 1998 and 1999.

The coefficient for the employment rate in equation (3) in Table 6.3 is estimated for all observations. There could be a large variation of the employment rate between the group and between the years. Therefore, we have estimated the equation for all groups and years separately and show the estimated coefficients for this variable in Table 6.4.

---

78 We have made the corresponding insertion in equation (3) in Table 6.3 recalculated in 1998 prices. The differences between the estimates based on the two equations are small.

TABLE 6.4.

Coefficient estimates of the effect of the rate of employment on the net transfer to public sector 1996, 1997 and 1998 for different groups

GROUP	COEFFICIENT ESTIMATES FOR THE EMPLOYMENT RATE IN 1996, 1997 AND 1998		
	1996	1997	1998
Born in Denmark			
Both parents born in Denmark	1.959	2.002	2.127
One parent born in Denmark, one in a Western country	1.808	1.877	1.887
One parent born in Denmark, one in a non-Western country	1.629	1.819	1.920
Both parents born in Western countries	2.022	2.182	2.001
Both parents born in non-Western countries	1.248	1.501	1.866
Born outside Denmark			
Born in a Western country	1.743	1.741	1.718
Born in a non-Western country	1.943	1.844	1.874

Note. The other independent variables included in the regressions, but for which estimates are not shown here, are age, age^2, female, and the family status variables.

We see that the values of the coefficients vary to some extent. The coefficients are higher for the Danish group (and for those with both parents born in a Western country), but the differences are rather small.[79] This means that an increase in the employment rate has more or less the same effect on the net redistribution whether we are considering a person born in Denmark with parents also born in Denmark, or a person born in a non-Western country. The estimated coefficients for the second generation of non-Western immigrants are considerably lower in 1996, however, which probably reflects that this is a group of young people and that the age variables that have been included do not eliminate the age effect completely. The value of that coefficient is higher in 1996 than in 1997 and higher in 1998 than in 1997, which probably is a result of changes in the age composition.

Next we will show the changes in the employment rate by age between 1996 and

---

79 The explanation for the relatively low values for the coefficients for those born in Western countries may be that it is more common in this group to have earnings paid by employers from outside of Denmark. ATP-fees are not paid on these earnings and they therefore do not influence the registered employment rate. As those earnings influence the taxes paid and the transfer payments received it means that we have people with zero employment rate but a positive net transfer to the public sector.

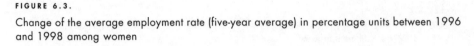

Change of the average employment rate (five-year average) in percentage units between 1996 and 1998 among women

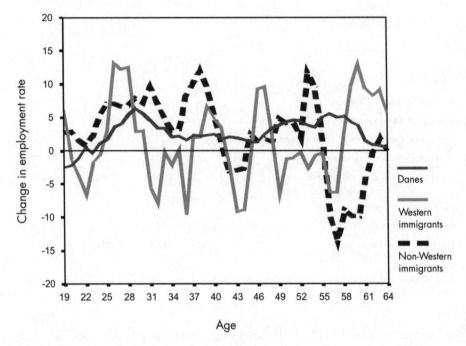

1998 for the three groups by means of two figures. Figure 6.3 shows the average change of employment rate by age for women and Figure 6.4 the corresponding information for men.

For Western immigrants we do not find any systematic differences between the two years. On the other hand, there is a small increase for Danes in some ages and a clear tendency of an increase for men from non-Western countries (for women the changes are harder to interpret).

6.4 The employment rate and net transfers

In sections 6.1 and 6.2 the great importance of the employment rate for the direction and size of the net transfer to the public sector has been shown. In section 6.3 the employment rate comparison between immigrants and Danes and the changes in that rate have been outlined. Now we will further consider the effects on the net transfers of variations in the employment rate. This will be done by showing the net transfers at three different rates of employment: the net transfers according to the actual employment rates (Figure 6.5), the net transfers for those who have an em-

FIGURE 6.4.

Change of the average employment rate (five-year average) in percentage units between 1996 and 1998 among men

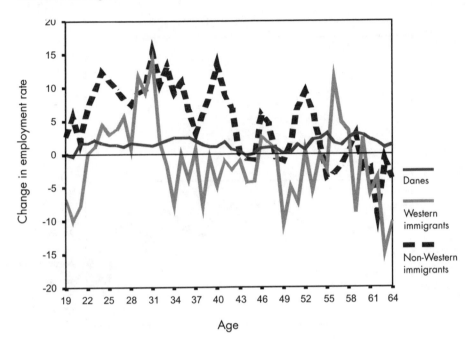

ployment rate of 100 per cent (Figure 6.6), and the net transfers for individuals who have an employment rate of zero (Figure 6.7). In the first case the whole population is taken into account, while in the other cases only those who have an employment rate of 100 or zero per cent, respectively, are observed. In the two latter cases, the age interval is limited to those of active age. In all cases, three groups are considered: Danes, Western immigrants and non-Western immigrants.

Figure 6.5 shows the net transfers by the actual rate of employment. It shows that the transfers vary by age, and that while there are small differences between Danes and Western immigrants, there are large differences between these two groups, on the one hand, and the immigrants from non-Western countries on the other. Regardless of age the non-Western immigrants receive on average a net transfer from the public sector. When examining the figure one should take into account that there are few older immigrants and consequently the average values are very sensitive for outliers. We have tried to reduce this problem first by using observations from 1996, 1997 and 1998, and second by calculating the values as three-year moving averages (the value for the age of 61 is an average of the values for the ages 60, 61 and 62). In Appendix Figures 6.A1 and 6.A2, corresponding estimates are shown for men and women, respectively. The general pattern is the same; that women have the main responsibility for childcare.

FIGURE 6.5.

Net transfer to the public sector per person (three-year average) in 1996, 1997 and 1998 for Danes, Western immigrants and non-Western immigrants (thousand Danish *kroner* in 1997 prices)

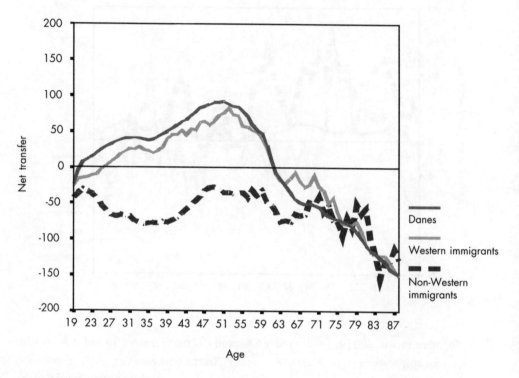

In the next step we will examine the net transfer for those who have an employment rate of 100, i.e., full-time and full year. We have limited the analysis to the age interval 19-64 since very few over the age of 64 have an employment rate that is 100 per cent and the average values then would be based on few observations. We find that the net transfers to the public sector are consistently positive for all of the three groups. It is also evident that the transfers are about the same size for Danes and Westerns immigrants but that they are remarkably lower for non-Western immigrants. It is clear that given the employment rate of 100, the transfers increase by age. One factor behind this may be that higher paid white-collar workers are remaining in the labour market longer than lower paid blue-collar workers. In Appendix Figures 6.A3 and 6.A4 corresponding estimates for men and women, respectively, are shown.

Now the question arises as to why the net transfers are lower from non-Western immigrants even when the employment rate is the same. We need more disaggregated information to answer this question. We have that information, not for every

FIGURE 6.6.

Net transfer to the public sector per person (three-year average) in 1996, 1997 and 1998 for Danes, Western immigrants and non-Western immigrants for those with 100 as employment rate (thousand Danish *kroner* in 1997 prices)

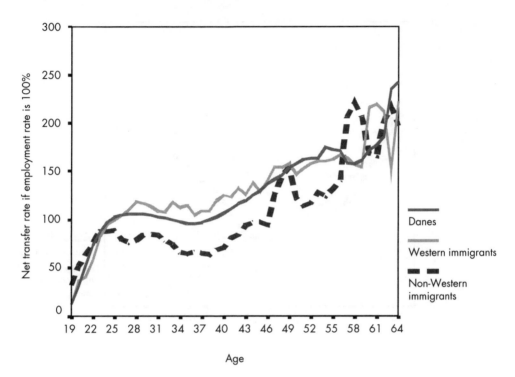

individual but for everyone with a certain rate of employment. We find that the explanation is that the costs for childcare and schooling are larger for these immigrants (they have more children) and that they pay less in taxes since they have lower incomes.

In Figure 6.7 a similar comparison is made for those who have a zero employment rate. On average the transfer goes from the public sector to all of the three groups. This is true for all ages. The transfers are smallest to Western immigrants and largest to non-Western immigrants, with the Danes in between.[80] The unusual shape of

---

80 A part of the explanation for the relatively low values of the coefficients for those born in Western countries may be that it is more common in this group to have earnings paid by employers from outside of Denmark. ATP-fees are not paid on these earnings and they therefore do not influence the registered employment rate. As those earnings influence the taxes paid and the transfer payments received, it means that we have people with zero employment rate but a positive net transfer to the public sector. See also the comments to Figure 7.3 and 7.4

FIGURE 6.7.

Net transfer to the public sector per person (three-year average) in 1996, 1997 and 1998 for Danes, Western immigrants and non-Western immigrants for those with 0 as employment rate (thousand Danish *kroner* in 1997 prices)

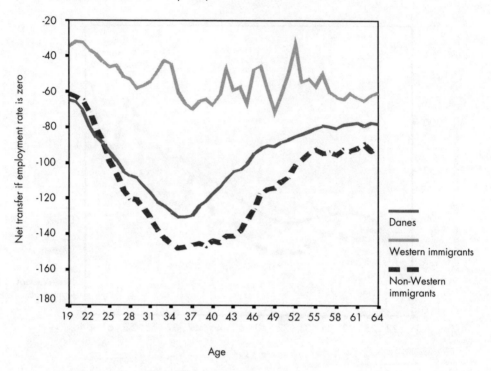

the curves with the largest transfers in the ages 30-45 is explained by many of these individuals having children who are under the age of 18. The pattern is the same, though not as clear, for those with the employment rate of 100 per cent. In Appendix Figures 6.A5 and 6.A6 corresponding estimates for men and women, respectively, are shown.

6.5 Conclusions

The variations in the individual net transfers to the public sector are large. As the immigrants constitute a small part of the population in Denmark, the major part of the variation is not between immigrants and Danes but within the Danish group. However, the net transfer to non-Western immigrants from the public sector is large per person. An introduction of demographic variables (gender, age, and family status) in the analysis increases the part of variation explained but does not reduce the value of a coefficient representing non-Western immigrants. However, if a variable representing the employment rate is introduced the part of the variation in net transfers explained increases considerably and the coefficient representing the non-Western immigrant group decreases drastically even if it is still significant. The effects of a change in the employment rate are more or less the same for the different groups as shown by separate regressions for each group. The employment rate increased between 1996 and 1998 especially for the non-Western groups, leading to less transfer to that group. The importance of the employment rate is also shown by presenting the net transfer for those with the actual, 100 and zero employment rates for the three groups (Danes, Western, non-Western). The differences are small between the three groups given the employment rate, which underlines its importance once again.

Appendix Tables to Chapter 6

TABLE 6.A1.

Regression estimates (OLS) with net transfers to the public sector in 1998 (in thousand Danish *kroner*) as dependent variable; and age, gender, family status, country of origin, length of stay in Denmark and employment rate as independent variables

VARIABLES	(1)	(2)	(3)
Constant	22.911 (0.414)	-139.086 (2.523)	-176.629 (2.077)
Born in Denmark			
Both parents born in Denmark	0	0	0
One parent born in Denmark, one in a Western country	9.320 (3.799)	-1.490 (3.394)	9.476 (2.788)
One parent born in Denmark, one in a non-Western country	3.130 (7.495)	-.348 (6.667)	18.443 (5.477)
Both parents born in a Western country	-3.570 (9.670)	-13.535 (8.581)	10.715 (7.049)
Both parents born in non-Western country	-23.658 (9.011)	-8.750 (8.025)	28.601 (6.594)
Born outside Denmark			
Born in a Western country			
Immigrated >12 years	-2.400 (3.673)	9.403 (3.266)	13.552 (2.683)
Immigrated 10-12	21.459 (13.997)	-8.571 (12.421)	19.406 (10.204)
Immigrated 7-10	-3.547 (11.516)	-30.218 (10.219)	8.831 (8.396)
Immigrated 5-7	13.225 (11.839)	-11.970 (10.506)	29.736 (8.632)
Immigrated 3-5	-7.199 (9.880)	-34.012 (8.769)	4.087 (7.205)
Immigrated 1-3	15.149 (7.995)	-4.291 (7.100)	58.264 (5.838)
Immigrated < 1 year	-3.247 (9.129)	-12.197 (8.110)	82.742 (6.672)
Born in a non-Western country			
Immigrated >12 years	-57.657 (3.377)	-77.595 (3.003)	-22.672 (2.476)
Immigrated 10-12	-103.348 (7.495)	-116.832 (6.656)	-34.452 (5.477)
Immigrated 7-10	-98.433 (5.547)	-105.731 (4.932)	-23.778 (4.064)

TABLE 6.A1. (continued)

TABLE 6.A1. (continued)

VARIABLES	(1)	(2)	(3)
Immigrated 5-7	-97.612 (6.895)	-103.757 (6.125)	-15.246 (5.043)
Immigrated 3-5	-99.498 (5.252)	-110.449 (4.669)	-12.219 (3.854)
Immigrated 1-3	-72.851 (5.761)	-81.824 (5.122)	7.510 (4.222)
Immigrated < 1 year	-48.898 (7.681)	-56.557 (6.825)	55.784 (5.623)
Female		-56.627 (0.716)	-33.428 (0.595)
Age		10.616 (0.113)	4.921 (0.095)
Age^2		-0.125 (0.001)	-0.048 (0.001)
Family status			
Unmarried, no children		0	0
Unmarried with children		-88.304 (2.271)	-98.200 (1.866)
Married, no children		33.780 (0.894)	15.405 (0.738)
Married with children		0.476 (1.012)	-41.885 (0.847)
Employment rate			2.067 (0.008)
N	139,701	139,701	139,701
R^2(adj)	0.011	0.221	0.474

Note. Standard errors in parentheses. Only persons 18 years and older are included. Married stands for living together irrespective of whether a couple is formally married or not.

TABLE 6.A2.

Regression estimates (OLS) with net transfers to the public sector (in thousand Danish *kroner* in 1997 prices) in 1996, 1997 and 1998 as dependent variable; and age, gender, family status, country of origin, length of stay in Denmark and employment rate as independent variables

VARIABLES	(1)	(2)	(3)
Constant	18.150 (0.398)	-134.767 (1.466)	-169.280 (1.213)
1997 sample	4.041 (0.556)	3.548 (0.496)	2.079 (0.410)
1998 sample	4.692 (0.555)	3.963 (0.496)	0.158 (0.410)
Born in Denmark			
Both parents born in Denmark	0	0	0
One parent born in Denmark, one in a Western country	9.206 (2.198)	-.018 (1.976)	11.318 (1.632)
One parent born in Denmark, one in a non-Western country	-2.964 (4.487)	-5.872 (4.015)	17.020 (3.316)
Both parents born in a Western country	5.829 (5.427)	-.900 (4.846)	12.144 (4.001)
Both parents born in non-Western country	-32.332 (5.453)	-18.872 (4.844)	16.148 (4.033)
Born outside Denmark			
Born in a Western country			
Immigrated >12 years	-6.538 (2.099)	5.614 (1.878)	10.858 (1.551)
Immigrated 10-12	-0.071 (9.324)	-25.939 (8.325)	4.810 (6.874)
Immigrated 7-10	-6.678 (6.747)	-31.113 (6.024)	5.308 (4.975)
Immigrated 5-7	2.402 (7.144)	-21.699 (6.378)	20.840 (5.268)
Immigrated 3-5	2.302 (6.130)	-21.101 (5.474)	16.689 (4.521)
Immigrated 1-3	4.064 (4.600)	-16.066 (4.110)	38.683 (3.3696)
Immigrated < 1 year	-18.451 (5.295)	-30.504 (4.732)	60.196 (3.913)

TABLE 6.A2. (continued)

TABLE 6.A2. (continued)

VARIABLES	(1)	(2)	(3)
Born in a non-Western country			
Immigrated >12 years	-59.414 (1.985)	-76.174 (1.775)	-24.472 (1.471)
Immigrated 10-12	-99.215 (4.313)	-116.558 (3.855)	-35.862 (3.189)
Immigrated 7-10	-97.658 (3.196)	-104.620 (2.858)	-23.209 (2.367)
Immigrated 5-7	-97.940 (3.864)	-102.075 (3.454)	-12.548 (2.859)
Immigrated 3-5	-99.010 (3.585)	-105.465 (3.205)	-6.573 (2.265)
Immigrated 1-3	-96.094 (3.051)	-106.553 (2.729)	-4.087 (2.265)
Immigrated < 1 year	-64.001 (4.326)	-70.982 (3.868)	44.731 (3.204)
Female		-55.409 (0.411)	-32.040 (0.343)
Age		10.125 (0.065)	4.632 (0.055)
Age^2		-0.120 (0.001)	-0.0045 (0.001)
Family status			
Unmarried, no children		0	0
Unmarried with children		-87.315 (1.288)	-95.457 (1.064)
Married, no children		32.497 (0.513)	14.801 (0.426)
Married with children		0.683 (0.580)	-40.042 (0.488)
Employment rate			2.015 (0.005)
N	417,376	417,376	417,376
R^2(adj)	0.012	0.212	0.463

Note. Standard errors in parentheses. Only persons 18 years and older are included. Married stands for living together irrespective of whether a couple is formally married or not.

Appendix Figures to Chapter 6

FIGURE 6.A1.

Net transfer to the public sector per person (three-year average) in 1996, 1997 and 1998 for Danes, Western immigrants and non-Western immigrants (thousand Danish *kroner* in 1997 prices). Men

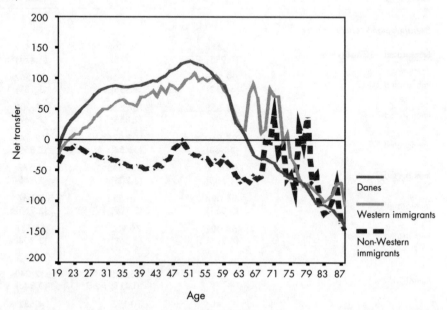

FIGURE 6.A2.

Net transfer to the public sector per person (three-year average) in 1996, 1997 and 1998 for Danes, Western immigrants and non-Western immigrants (thousand Danish *kroner* in 1997 prices). Women

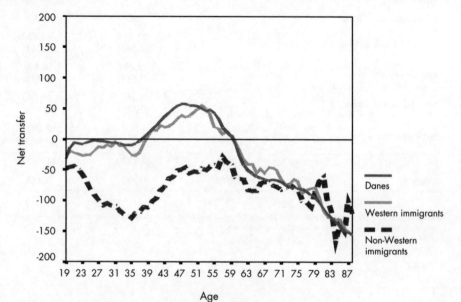

FIGURE 6.A3.

Net transfer to the public sector per person (three-year average) in 1996, 1997 and 1998 for Danes, Western immigrants and non-Western immigrants for those with 100 as employment rate (thousand Danish *kroner* in 1997 prices). Men

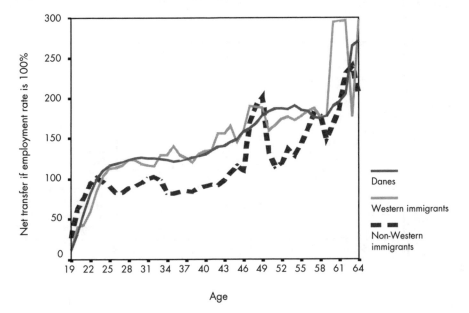

FIGURE 6.A4.

Net transfer to the public sector per person (three-year average) in 1996, 1997 and 1998 for Danes, Western immigrants and non-Western immigrants for those with 100 as employment rate (thousand Danish *kroner* in 1997 prices). Women

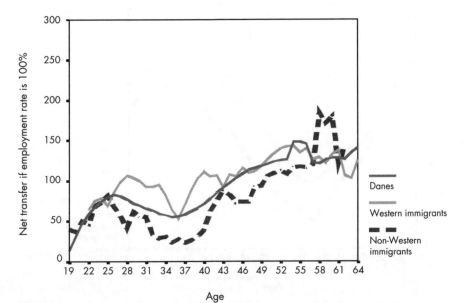

FIGURE 6.A5.

Net transfer to the public sector per person (three-year average) in 1996, 1997 and 1998 for Danes, Western immigrants and non-Western immigrants for those with 0 as employment rate (thousand Danish *kroner* in 1997 prices). Men

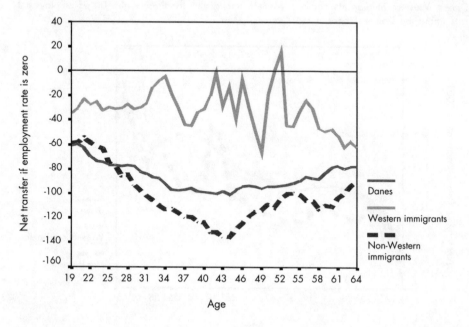

FIGURE 6.A6.

Net transfer to the public sector per person (three-year average) in 1996, 1997 and 1998 for Danes, Western immigrants and non-Western immigrants for those with 0 as employment rate (thousand Danish *kroner* in 1997 prices). Women

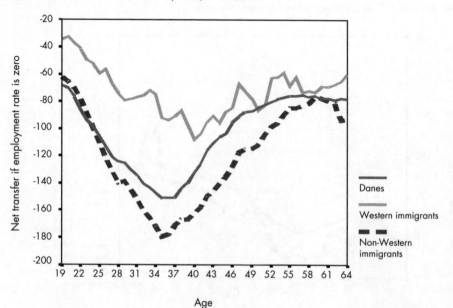

Chapter 7
A Life-cycle Analysis
Based on Individual Data

Chapters 5 and 6 are based on cross sectional data and show the redistribution that takes place during a given year. For different reasons, such an analysis can be misleading when we want to draw conclusions about the total effects of immigration during a certain year. First, the state of the labour market may influence the result. For example, if we examine a year with high unemployment, this year might not be representative for all years when it comes to the extent of the net transfers. Using cross sectional data from several years can partly solve this problem. Second, variations in the extent of the immigration might be of importance. If there are many immigrants one year the redistribution this year and the years following might be larger if it takes time before the immigrants become established in the labour market. To some extent, controlling for the length of stay in the country and comparing immigrants with different lengths of stay can solve this problem. However, different cohorts can differ with respect to the composition of, for example, education or country of origin. Third, it is possible that immigrants arrive in the country at an age when they are likely to have relatively many children per adult person. With the method we have used in Chapter 6, the costs for the coming generation are assigned to the adult generation. It would be more correct to treat every individual separately, the children included, in order to follow the income transfers over the life cycle.

In this chapter the total effect of immigrants of different ages on the public sector is presented. Calculations are also presented of the effect on the public sector of the actual size and age composition of immigration.

In the previous chapters, individual public consumption in relation to children under 18 years of age is assigned to the parents, and transfers to adults according to their parenthood are also assigned to the parents. This means that the calculated net transfers per person over 18 years of age concern both these people and a part of the coming generation (children under the age of 18 years). These children were either born in a foreign country and immigrated with their parents, or were born in Denmark. Hence, this group of children consists of both first and second-generation immigrants.

For two reasons it may be inappropriate to assign net transfers for children to the parents' net transfers. First, the amounts are distributed per person over 18 years of age and not per person; a distribution per person would give a lower amount on average since the total net transfer is distributed on more individuals. This also changes the relative level between the groups since the number of children per adult differs between groups (it is highest among the non-Western immigrants). This is easy to adjust but does not solve the second problem, which is that the calculations cover two generations.

The calculations refer to combinations of two generations, as mentioned. A part of the explanation for the high transfers to non-Western immigrants is that many in this group are of an age when people are parents to children under 18 years old. Also, given the age composition, non-Western immigrants have a rather high rate of fertility.[81] It would be better if we were able to study the transfer over the life cycle and not have the children's costs added to the parents' costs. A first step is to study the net transfers to the first generation over the life cycle and then study the second and following generations.

To do an analysis that focuses on the first generation we need to remove the part of the net transfer that belongs to the second generation. We have performed these calculations in two ways. First, in section 7.1, we have used an indirect method where both information about certain parts of the transfer system and information from regression estimations of the remaining public costs have been the basis for calculating the first generation's net transfers without the costs for the second generation (the children) included. Such indirect estimates have been calculated for 1996, 1997 and 1998.[82] For 1995 and 1998 there is also data that is already corrected for this, so that public expenses are distributed to all individuals, including those 17 years or younger. This means that we can calculate the average net transfers without having to apply the indirect method. We call these estimates the direct estimates and present the results in section 7.2.

7.1 Net transfers over the life cycle: An indirect estimation method

In this section the indirect estimation method is presented. We start from the version of the Law Model where the costs for children are assigned to the parents. The aim is to separate the net transfers to children from those to their parents.

First of all, there are transfers that are directed towards families and single parents with children. We can calculate the size of these transfers for the individuals in our sample by using information about the transfer system and the number of children.

---

81   See, e.g., Ejby Poulsen & Lange (1998); and Chapter 1 in Viby Mogensen & Matthiessen (2000).
82   In Wadensjö (2000a) the indirect method is used for 1996 and 1997. When that study was made the data necessary for the direct method was not available.

The subsidy to families with children in 1996 was 10,200 Danish *kroner* for children 0-2 years old, 9,100 *kroner* for 3-6 year old children and 7,100 *kroner* for the children 7-17 years old. In 1997 the corresponding amounts were 10,500, 9,400 and 7,400 *kroner* and in 1998 11,000, 10,000 and 7,800 *kroner*. In the Law Model, the subsidy is assigned to the mother when the parents are married. When it comes to single parents, the subsidies go to the parent who has custody of the child. Moreover, single parents received a subsidy of 4,500 per child and also 3,500 *kroner* irrespective of the number of children. In 1998 these subsidies were 4,644 and 3,548 *kroner* respectively.[83]

The costs for individual public consumption for married parents are equally distributed on both parents in the Law Model. For single parents, they are assigned to the parent who has custody. The most important costs are childcare and schooling, but there are also costs for medical services, etc. We do not have information on the extent of these costs for each individual.[84]

Also, the incidence of children affects the taxes paid by the household. Transfers to families with children lead to increased consumption and hence to more indirect tax payments. Having children might also affect the individual's labour supply and earnings and as a consequence what they pay in income taxes and indirect taxes. It is not self-evident how these effects on taxes shall be distributed over the first and second generation, which means that it is not clear how the net transfer of a household should be distributed over the first and second generation.

We do not have direct information about the extent of the net transfers to children for 1996 and 1997. We will therefore make estimations partially based on other information available for those two years. Although we have direct information, we shall use here the same indirect method for 1998 in order to make it possible to compare the two methods.

The calculations according to the indirect method are done in several steps. We start from regression estimates based on individual information from 1996, 1997 and 1998 where the net transfers depend, among other things, on employment rate, age, immigrant group, and family status (married or single) and for every kind of family status a division depending on the number of children (0,1,2,3,4 or more).

---

83   The Ministry of Economic Affairs has provided the above subsidy figures.

84   We have, however, information about costs for childcare and teaching for each group (Danes, non-Western immigrants etc.) and consequently we could calculate the costs for childcare per child under 18 years of age. We cannot do this for education, however, since a considerable part of the education costs refers to people over 18 years old and we cannot separate this part. Another example of information available is that the cost for hospital care was 1,570 *kroner* per child in 1997 and the cost for medical service and medicine was 850 *kroner* per child in the same year.

The employment rate is included in order to try to eliminate the effect of the change in the household's labour supply.[85]

We inspect the coefficient estimates for every type of family status with different numbers of children; i.e., we compare the coefficient for married women with one child with married women with no children, married women with two children with married women with one child, etc. This gives an estimation of the difference in net transfers that is explained by a child.[86] In the next step we reduce these amounts by the amounts of transfers concerning the children and use our information about the redistribution system.[87] We then receive adjusted values for the coefficients that refer to components – other than transfers – in the net redistribution. After that, the values for married people are multiplied by two in order to get the effect on public consumption (and to some extent, taxes) per child. We then get a number of values for net transfers exclusive of the transfers to their children. We calculate the average of these values and find that the average was 47,600 *kroner* in 1996, 49,900 in 1997 and 55,800 in 1998 (the full amount per child to single parents and half the amount to married parents since, in that case, the amount is shared by the parents). The values of transfers and individual public consumption calculated in this way are approximately at the same level that Wallberg, Medelberg & Strömqvist (1996) got using another method. We use these average values and information about the direct transfers to calculate the net transfers to adults where we have removed the net transfers that concern the next generation. Table 7.1 and 7.2 show the revised amounts together with the unrevised.

Table 7.1 shows both the calculations made for 1996, 1997 and 1998 that were previously shown in Table 5.3 and the values received when the net transfers to children under 18 years old are eliminated. We see that the average net transfers *to* the public sector increase by 15,000 *kroner* for 1996 and 1997, and by about 18,000 *kroner* for 1998, after this recalculation. However, the differences between the groups are considerable. The effect is greatest for the non-Western immigrants. For non-Western immigrants transfers *from* the public sector are reduced by 34,000, 33,000 and 37,000 *kroner,* respectively, for the years 1996-1998. This reflects the age compo-

---

85   Since the employment rate is not exact, the whole effect is not eliminated.

86   Since we use coefficient estimates that refer to all households with children – Danes as well as immigrants – we do not take into account that the net transfers might be higher for immigrants' children. A study performed by Indenrigsministeriet (1998) shows that the costs for a child in elementary school are somewhat higher for immigrant children from non-Western countries than for Danish children.

87   We have not taken into account that a part of the transfers is paid back to the public sector in the form of indirect taxes.

TABLE 7.1.

Net transfers to the public sector (in Danish *kroner*) per person 18 years and older for different groups (with or without revision of net transfers to children) in 1996, 1997 and 1998. (Amounts in 1997 prices in parentheses)

GROUP	1996	1996 (REV)	1997	1997 (REV)	1998	1998 (REV)
Danish population (excluding those who have one immigrant parent)	18,600 (19,000)	32,300 (33,000)	22,700	37,100	24,600 (24,100)	41,400 (40,700)
Danish population (including those who have one immigrant parent)	18,700 (19,100)	32,500 (33,200)	22,800	37,200	24,700 (24,200)	41,600 (40,100)
Second generation – one Danish parent and one immigrant parent from a Western country	29,600 (30,200)	47,000 (48,800)	31,000	49,300	32,200 (31,600)	55,600 (54,600)
Second generation – one Danish parent and one immigrant parent from a non-Western country	12,400 (12,700)	22,300 (22,800)	19,000	32,700	26,000 (25,500)	41,300 (40,500)
Second generation – two parents from Western countries	27,500 (28,100)	47,300 (48,300)	34,400	52,400	19,300 (18,900)	41,200 (40,400)
Immigrants from Western countries	10,900 (11,100)	25,300 (25,900)	13,000	28,300	23,800 (23,400)	39,600 (38,900)
Immigrants from Western countries (first and second generation)	12,300 (12,600)	27,100 (27,700)	14,700	30,300	23,500 (23,000)	39,700 (39,000)
Second generation – two parents from non-Western countries	-11,600 (-11,800)	-8,900 (-9,100)	-13,100	-11,000	-700 (-700)	8,000 (7,900)
Immigrants from non-Western countries	-66,000 (-67,400)	-32,400 (-33,100)	-60,300	-27,300	-54,500 (-53,500)	-17,200 (-16,900)
Immigrants from non-Western countries (first and second generation)	-63,700 (-65,000)	-31,400 (-32,100)	-58,200	-26,500	-51,900 (-50,900)	-16,000 (-15,700)
Total	15,000 (15,300)	30,000 (30,700)	19,500	34,600	21,500 (21,000)	39,200 (38,500)

Note: Western countries are EU countries, Norway, Switzerland, Iceland, North America, Australia and New Zealand; non-Western countries are all other countries.

sition among this group (many of them are at an age where it is common to have minor children) and given this age composition, that the group has relatively many children. Still, the net transfer goes from the public sector to the non-Western immigrants. The net transfers change more than average for the second generation of Western immigrants, which again is due to the age composition (many of them have

TABLE 7.2.

Net transfers to the public sector (in Danish *kroner*) per person 18 years and older from non-Western countries according to length of stay in Denmark (with or without revision of net transfers to children) in 1996, 1997 and 1998. (Amounts in 1997 prices in parentheses)

LENGTH OF STAY*	1996	1996 (REV)	1997	1997 (REV)	1998	1998 (REV)
Less than one year	-55,800 (-57,000)	-32,700 (-33,400)	-45,500	-28,500	-26,000 (25,000)	-5,800 (-5,700)
1-3 years	-89,900 (-91,800)	-62,900 (-64,300)	-79,900	-49,900	-49,900 (-49,000)	-22,000 (-21,600)
3-5 years	-79,300 (-81,000)	-45,500 (-46,500)	-78,300	-40,600	-76,600 (-75,200)	-38,500 (-37,800)
5-7 years	-83,600 (-85,400)	-44,500 (-45,500)	-71,500	-33,500	-74,700 (-73,300)	-31,700 (-31,100)
7-10 years	-82,100 (-83,800)	-39,900 (-40,800)	-70,500	-32,700	-75,500 (-74,100)	-25,500 (-25,000)
10 years or more	-46,700 (-47,700)	-12,700 (-13,000)	-46,000	-12,700	-42,400 (-41,600)	-5,000 (-5,000)
Second generation	-11,600 (-11,800)	-9,000 (-9,200)	-13,100	-11,000	-700 (-700)	8,000 (7,900)
Total	-63,700 (-65,000)	-31,400 (-32,100)	-58,200	-26,500	-51,900 (-50,100)	-16,000 (-15,700)

*The division according to length of stay is based on exact age. 'Less than one year' in the column for the year 1996 includes those who immigrated on 1 January 1996 or later, '1-3 years' includes those who immigrated between 1 January 1994 and 31 December 1995, etc.

children 17 years or younger). On the other hand the transfers to the second generation of non-Western immigrants are only reduced to a small extent. This is a very young group (the greater part is between 18 and 30 years old) and few of them have children of their own.

Table 7.1 shows that even if we removed a part of the net transfers to children, the net transfers still go *from* the public sector to the immigrants from non-Western countries. This result is driven by the low employment rate among immigrants from these countries. We know that the employment rate varies with the length of residency in Denmark. Therefore, we will show the corresponding recalculations with a division into length of residency for the non-Western immigrants, see Table 7.2. The result is that the reduction varies somewhat by the length of residency. Those who have lived in Denmark less than one year have fewer children. However, we also see that the net transfers according to the recalculated values in every length-of-residency category go from the public sector to the immigrants. For those immigrants who have spent 10 years or more in Denmark the amount was 12,700 *kroner* in 1997.

In the appendix figures to this chapter, the variation in net transfers over the life cycle for those aged 18 and over are shown using the indirect method for eliminating the net transfer to those aged 17 and younger from the net transfer of their parents. In Appendix Figure 7.A1-3 the results are shown for all, irrespective of the employment rate; in Figure 7.A4-6 the results for those with full employment; and in Figure 7.A5-7 those with an employment rate of zero. As the results are very similar to those shown in the next section, based on the direct estimation method, the results are not commented upon further here.

TABLE 7.3.

Net transfers to the public sector (in Danish *kroner*) per person 18 years and older for different groups in 1998, excluding the net transfer to children according to two different methods, and 1995 according to the direct estimate method. (Amounts in 1998 prices in parentheses)

GROUP	INDIRECT ESTIMATE 1998	DIRECT ESTIMATE 1998	DIRECT ESTIMATE 1995
Danish population (excluding those with one immigrant parent)	41,400	38,300	27,000 (28,800)
Danish population (including those with one immigrant parent)	41,600	38,500	27,100 (28,900)
Second generation – one Danish parent and one immigrant parent from a Western country	55,600	51,700	34,600 (36,900)
Second generation – one Danish parent and one immigrant parent from a non-Western country	41,300	40,100	26,100 (27,800)
Second generation – two parents from Western countries	41,200	36,500	*
Immigrants from Western countries	39,600	35,700	26,100 (27,800)
Immigrants from Western countries (first and second generation)	39,700	35,800	26,300 (28,000)
Second generation – two parents from non-Western countries	8,000	5,600	*
Immigrants from non-Western countries	-17,200	-27,200	-83,600 (-89,100)
Immigrants from non-Western countries (first and second generation)	-16,000	-25,700	-58,900 (-62,800)
Total	39,200	35,800	25,200 (26,800)

Note: Western countries are EU countries, Norway, Switzerland, Iceland, North America, Australia and New Zealand; non-Western countries are all other countries.

* = few observations.

7.2 Net transfers over the life cycle: A direct estimation method

For 1998 and also 1995 another method is possible to use, as mentioned in the introduction to this chapter. This method is based on the Law Model where public expenditure is distributed directly over all individuals, including children. In this section we will focus on the adults. In Table 7.3, the indirect and the direct estimates for 1998 are shown together with the direct estimates for 1995. The indirect estimates for 1998 are the ones previously presented in Table 7.1.

When comparing the direct and indirect estimates for 1998 in Table 7.3, it is clear that the direct estimates, which are based on more accurate information, are lower than the indirect estimates, i.e. the net transfers are on average lower according to the direct method. A too large net transfer is ascribed to the children if the indirect method is used. Comparing the direct estimates for 1995 and 1998, net transfers have become more positive over time (and much less negative for the non-Western immigrants), which is in accordance with previous results concerning the change in net transfers between 1995 and 1998.

The values according to the direct estimation method for 1998 are also shown in Figure 7.1-7.3 with the average net transfer by age for the three groups: Danes, Western immigrants and non-Western immigrants. This is done in three cases: for all (i.e., the actual rate of employment), for those with the employment rate 100 per cent and for those with the employment rate zero. The figures can be compared to Figure 6.5-6.7.

Some observations should be noted. First of all, it is obvious that all curves are shifted upwards (compared to Figure 6.5-6.7). The explanation is that the net transfers directed to children are eliminated. Second, Figure 7.1 shows that at the actual employment rate, there are no net transfers at any age from non-Western immigrants of active age to the public sector (between 45 and 50 years of age the net transfers are close to zero).[88] Third, we see that the particular shape of the curves in Figure 6.5-6.7, which is due to the high number of parents in certain age groups, is not found in Figure 7.1-7.3. Fourth, we see that the curves for the three groups differ in a systematic way. At the actual employment rate the curves for Danes and the Western immigrants are close to each other while the curve for the non-Western group is far below. About the same pattern is seen when the employment rate is 100 per cent, even if the difference in *kroner* is smaller. At the employment rate zero the pattern is different. The net transfers to Danes and non-Western immigrants are on about the same level while the transfers to Western immigrants are much smaller.

---

88   The exception for those 70 years old is due to the fact that there are few in that age group, and among them some people with very high incomes.

FIGURE 7.1.

Net transfer to the public sector per person (three-year average; thousand Danish *kroner*) in 1998 for Danes, Western immigrants and non-Western immigrants. For all independent of the employment rate. Net transfers to children under 18 are not included

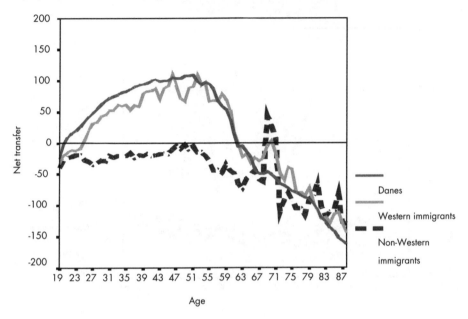

FIGURE 7.2.

Net transfer to the public sector per person (three-year average; thousand Danish *kroner*) in 1998 for Danes, Western immigrants and non-Western immigrants. For those with 100 as employment rate. Net transfers to children under 18 are not included

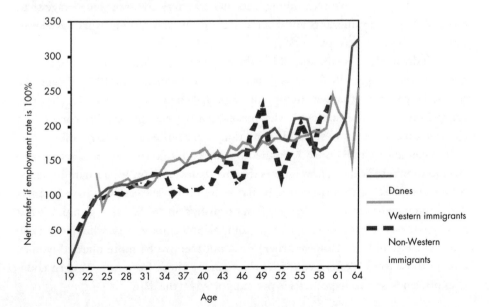

FIGURE 7.3.

Net transfer to the public sector per person (three-year average; thousand Danish *kroner*) in 1998 for Danes, Western immigrants and non-Western immigrants. For those with 0 as employment rate. Net transfers to children under 18 are not included

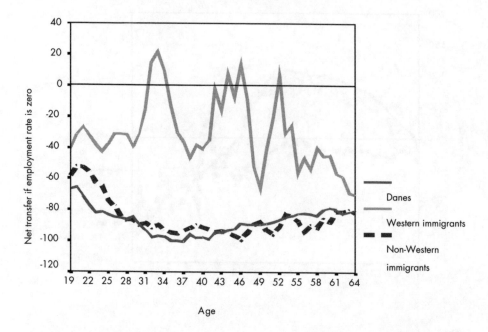

In Figure 6.6 (a figure which also shows the net transfers for those with full employment) there are some differences between the groups, but these differences are smaller here. Still, the non-Western immigrants' net transfers are lower on average than those of Western immigrants and Danes. The non-Western immigrants have lower wages and therefore pay less in taxes.

For individuals 55 years and older, the curves for the immigrant groups show great variation, especially for those with an employment rate of 100 per cent. We should keep in mind that few immigrants, especially non-Western, have reached this age and even fewer are employed. This means that the averages in these parts of the curves are based on few observations and that coincidences play a large role.

In accordance with Figure 6.7, Figure 7.3 points out that the net transfers are considerably lower to Western immigrants than to Danes and non-Western immigrants. A first hypothesis is that there is a greater share of housewives, who have partners with high incomes and hence receive fewer transfers, in the Western group. We test this hypothesis by examining the family composition among those who have an employment rate of zero. However, there does not seem to be more married women among those from Western countries than among those from non-Western countries or Danes, so this hypothesis is not supported by the data.

FIGURE 7.4.

Net transfer to the public sector per person (three-year average; thousand Danish *kroner*) in 1998 for Danes, Western immigrants and non-Western immigrants. For those with 0 as employment rate excluding those with earnings greater than 100,000 Danish *kroner*. Net transfers to children under 18 are not included

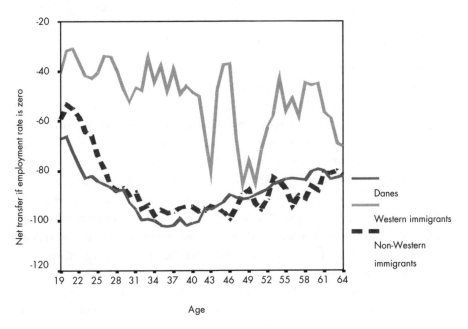

A second hypothesis is that some of the people in the Western group are employed and get their salary from employers outside Denmark and therefore neither earnings nor employment are registered. Such a group will receive no – or very small – income transfers and the net transfers from the public sector consequently become small given the registered employment rate (mostly some forms of individual public consumption). This is probably a group that has recently arrived in Denmark for a short stay in the country. This hypothesis gets some support. Relatively many of those who have the employment rate zero, and who come from Western countries, arrived only a few years before 1998 and have lower net transfers on average than those who arrived earlier and also have the employment rate zero.

We have tested this hypothesis further by looking at those who have a zero employment rate but positive earnings. There may be several explanations for this combination, for example the fact that people who have become unemployed or have left the labour force first receive their vacation payments the following year. To avoid any ambiguity with the various types of delayed payment, we have set an earnings limit of 100,000 Danish *kroner* and have eliminated those with earnings exceeding that level from the group with a zero employment rate. Of those with a zero employment rate, 1.17 per cent of Western immigrants had earnings exceeding 100,000 Danish *kroner*, but only 0.26 of the Danes and 0.32 of the non-Western immigrants.[89] As seen in Figure 7.4 the net transfers to the public sector are now negative also for Western immigrants with a zero employment rate, but still not as low as for the other two groups.

7.3 The total net transfers over the life cycle[90]

We will now try to estimate the total redistribution over the lifecycle for an individual of Western or non-Western origin who immigrates into Denmark at some age. This has been done in two different ways for two age intervals. In the age interval 0-67 years information about average net transfers for each group is used. For individuals 68 years and older the average values for the Danes are used for all groups since the number of observations is small for the immigrant groups and random variation would play too large a role if the actual values were used.[91] We use data from 1998 that makes it possible to use the direct method, i.e., the costs for a child are deducted from the parent's net transfer already in the Law Model. We see these estimations as a first step towards more realistic estimations where the assimilation process will be modelled and where the level of the curve differs because of the age when the individual arrives in Denmark.[92]

We start with Figure 7.5, which shows transfers for people of different ages. The results differ between the two groups of immigrants. For the Western immigrants we find the traditional pattern where the transfer goes *to* the public sector from people of active age and *from* the public sector to those of non-active age (children, the elderly). The figure might give the impression that the total transfers over the life cycle from this group will go from the public sector since the net transfers to the elderly are high (the care costs are high).[93] However, there are only a small number of individuals who live that long and consequently the high costs per person do not have

---

89 The difference is even more pronounced if we set the limit to more than 200,000 Danish *kroner*. The percentages are 1.01, 0.08 and 0.10, respectively.

90 Concerning Sweden, see a corresponding calculation in Storesletten (1998).

91 Many elderly immigrants in Denmark arrived when they were rather old to join younger family members. In the future this group will not make up any dominating share of older immigrants in Denmark.

92 A method applied on immigration to the USA is generational accounting, see Auerbach & Oroupoulos (1999, 1999a). This method would be possible to apply in a future study on Denmark.

93 The transfer payments (pensions) are on the same level irrespective of age for those 65 and older. However, average costs for care of the elderly increase with age.

FIGURE 7.5.

Net transfer to the public sector according to age (three-year average), in thousand Danish *kroner*, in 1998

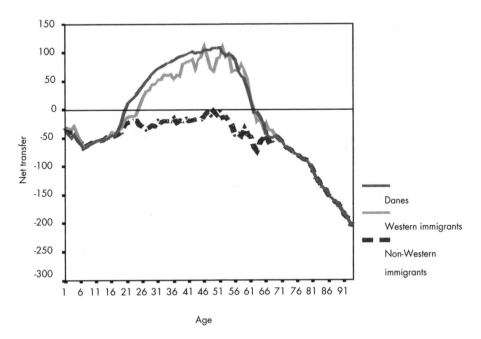

Age

Note. Average values for each group 0-67 years and the same values as for the Danes for those 68 years and older.

as much influence as the figure leads us to believe. For non-Western immigrants on the other hand, the net transfers are always negative. This should not be interpreted, though, as what the net transfers look like for one single person over the life cycle. Those who arrive when they are very young (before school age) might find it easier to establish themselves on the labour market than those who arrive as adults.

Figure 7.6 shows the net transfers in 1998 just as Figure 7.5, but only for those aged 0-17. The purpose is to make the pattern more visible. The differences between the groups of children are not as large as those for the adults and the net transfers are overall negative as expected, with a large drop around the age when they start school.[94] The transfer to the Danish children is slightly higher in the age group 2-5 years, most likely a result of the fact that Danish children are in public day-care centres to a higher extent than immigrant children.

---

94 Compare with the results in Wallberg, Medelberg & Strömqvist (1996), p. 52.

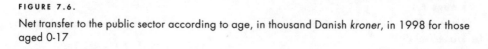

FIGURE 7.6.

Net transfer to the public sector according to age, in thousand Danish *kroner*, in 1998 for those aged 0-17

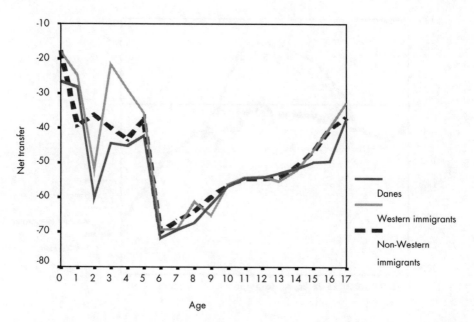

The next step is to estimate the total net transfer over the life cycle for individuals who arrive at different ages. Here we must take mortality rates and the re-emigration propensity for each group into consideration, otherwise high ages will be given too much significance. We have therefore used information about the mortality at different ages. Regarding the re-emigration, we have used information about immigrants from EU countries for the Western immigrants and information about immigrants from Asia for the non-Western immigrants.[95]

Figure 7.7 shows the values for immigrants from Western and non-Western countries. For every age, the amount of the net transfer shown in the figure is the total net transfer over the remainder of the life cycle for an individual immigrating at that age. As a comparison there is a level for Danes, who, in a manner of speaking, 'immigrate' at the age of zero (the amount assigns to the age of zero but in order to make the comparison easier there is a line). In the calculations we have assumed that there is no emigration of Danes[96]. Since the transfers in all age groups go from the public sec-

---

95   Concerning the mortality and re-emigration numbers, see Statistics Denmark (2000).

96   The number of Danes who migrate from Denmark is rather small and therefore we do not consider this simplifying assumption to be a major problem.

FIGURE 7.7.

Total net transfer to the public sector at immigration at different ages; as a comparison the value for Danes (who 'immigrate' at age 0) is shown as a horizontal line. Values for 1998 in thousand Danish *kroner*; discount rate = 0 per cent

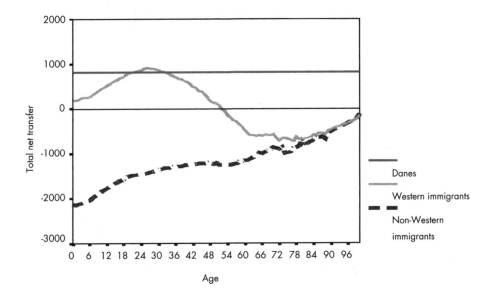

tor to the non-Western immigrants, the total transfers become smaller the higher the age at immigration. For Western immigrants the total net transfers to the public sector are large and positive if they arrive at the usual age of labour force entrance.

We can expect that the net transfers will change over time with the growth of the economy. This accounts for taxes and transfers as well as for public consumption, and indicates that the amounts for the later years should be adjusted upwards. On the other hand, there are reasons for discounting future amounts (we prefer one *krone* now compared to one *krone* in the future). In Figure 7.7 the amounts are not discounted but, on the other hand, there is no adjustment upwards of the amounts either. This can be interpreted as though the economic growth and the discount factor are assumed to be equal. But this is not necessarily the case. In order to test the sensitivity for different assumptions we have also calculated the cases with a discount factor of 1 per cent, 2 per cent and 3.5 per cent. Figure 7.8 shows the case with a discount factor of 3.5 per cent.[97] The shifts are remarkable. The transfer for Danes also becomes negative when using this discount factor.

---

97   This is the same discount factor that Storesletten (1998) uses.

FIGURE 7.8.

Total net transfer to the public sector at immigration at different ages; as a comparison the value for Danes (who 'immigrate' at age 0) is shown as a horizontal line. Values for 1998 in thousand Danish *kroner*; discount rate = 3.5 per cent

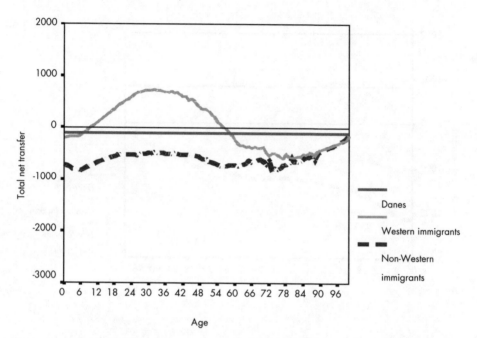

To point out the importance of the discount rate, Table 7.4 shows the total net transfers over the life cycle if immigrating at age zero, using four different discount rates. Two of them, 0 and 3.5 per cent, were used in the Figures 7.7 and 7.8, respectively.

Table 7.4 shows that the size of the total net transfers decreases the higher the discount rate. Assumptions on the future economic development are therefore of great importance for the size of the net transfers. The total net transfer over the life cycle from a non-Western immigrant is negative regardless of the discount rate used, in contrast to the net transfer from a Dane or a Western immigrant whose net transfers are positive or just below zero. However, there is a great improvement if the values for 1998 are used compared to those for 1995.

So far in this section we have shown the effects on net transfers of first generation immigrants, i.e., those born outside Denmark and whose parents were not born in Denmark. The results show that irrespective of age, there is redistribution to non-Western immigrants and that this redistribution is considerable. This result depends to a large extent on the low employment rate, if the employment rate increases the result changes. We are going to show this below using some examples. We will examine how large the total net transfers become if the non-Western immigrants of active

TABLE 7.4.

Total net transfers over the life cycle to the public sector from an immigrant who immigrated to Denmark in 1998 aged 0 years (and for a Danish child born in Denmark), in thousand Danish *kroner*. Corresponding values for immigration in 1995 are in parentheses

DISCOUNT RATE (%)	DANES	IMMIGRANTS FROM WESTERN COUNTRIES	IMMIGRANTS FROM NON-WESTERN COUNTRIES
0	814 (334)	185 (30)	-2134 (-3146)
1	505 (226)	18 (-29)	-1385 (-2135)
2	207 (57)	-99 (-94)	-1017 (-1532)
3.5	-109 (-151)	-207 (-160)	-708 (-1017)

age have an employment rate that is 10 percentage points higher than the one they had in 1998 and also if they have the same employment rate as the Danes in that year. We use two discount factors, 0 and 3.5 per cent, in Figures 7.9 and 7.10, respectively. We see that at the same employment rate as for the Danish group, the sum of net transfers to the public sector turns positive if immigration takes place some time between 0 and about 45 years of age at the discount rate 0, and between 10 and about 55 years at the discount rate 3.5 per cent.

FIGURE 7.9.

Total net transfers to the public sector at immigration at different ages for non-Western immigrants with three different assumptions regarding employment rate. Values for 1998 in thousand Danish *kroner*; discount rate = 0 per cent

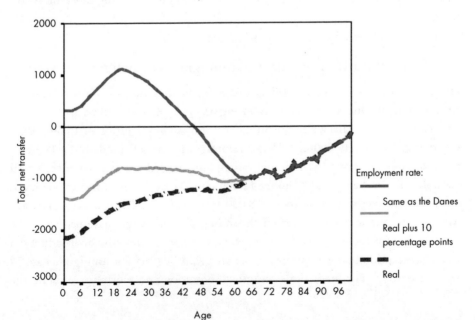

FIGURE 7.10.

Total net transfers to the public sector at immigration at different ages for non-Western immigrants with three different assumptions regarding employment rate. Values for 1998 in thousand Danish *kroner;* discount rate = 3.5 per cent

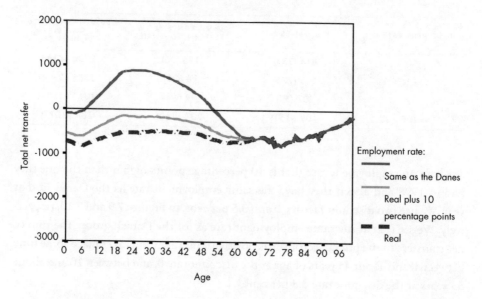

We have assumed that the employment rate at a certain age is independent of the age at which the immigration took place. However, it is more realistic to see the net transfer as dependent on both the length of residency in Denmark and the age when immigration took place. Therefore it is important to proceed using this kind of analysis.

7.4 The total net transfer effect of immigrants arriving in one year

The preceding analysis can be used as a basis for further analysis of the total long-term net transfer due to immigration during one year. Here we will see the expected total effects on net transfers to the public sector of an immigration of 10,000 Western immigrants and 10,000 non-Western immigrants in 1998 (and 1995). These figures do not correspond to the actual values, but should be seen as an arithmetical example only. In the year 2000, about 12,000 non-Danish people came to Denmark from Western countries and about 18,000 from non-Western countries. The age structure (in one-year age groups) of the immigrants arriving is assumed to be the same as that for the immigrants of the respective two groups who arrived in 1998 with the exception that we assume that all are below 70 (very few immigrants are 70 years or older).[98] The predictions on return migration and mortality rates are the

TABLE 7.5.

Total net transfers to the public sector in million Danish *kroner* due to an immigration of 10,000 people from Western and 10,000 from non-Western countries in 1998. The age structure is the same as that of the actual immigration from the two groups in that year (excluding immigrants aged 70 years and older). Corresponding values for immigration in 1995 are in parentheses

DISCOUNT RATE (%)	IMMIGRANTS FROM WESTERN COUNTRIES	IMMIGRANTS FROM NON-WESTERN COUNTRIES
0	6,718 (4,152)	-15,446 (-26,027)
1	6,314 (4,349)	-11,062 (-19,187)
2	5,697 (4,059)	-8,325 (-14,904)
3.5	4,717 (3,482)	-5,864 (-10,882)

same as before. It is important to note that the figures represent the lifetime effect on net transfer to the public sector and not the effect for a single year.

The numbers shown in Table 7.5 are quite large and indicate that the effects of immigration on the public sector are quite considerable. The effects on the net transfer as a result of immigration from Western countries are large and positive. The explanation is that the majority of the immigrants arrive at young adult age, the employment rate is high and the return migration is considerable (many leave before retirement). For the non-Western group the net transfer to the immigrants is large. Like the Western immigrants, the non-Western immigrants are mainly young adults but they are employed to a lesser extent. The fact that these figures are large shows the importance of making it easier in different ways for immigrants to enter the labour market. The effects of a generally better labour market situation are seen if the figures for 1995 and 1998 are compared. The calculated total net transfers to the non-Western immigrants are much lower in the 1998 calculation and the total net transfer from the Western immigrants to the public sector are still higher. As previously seen in section 7.3, the discount rate plays an important role for the size of the amounts.

7.5 Conclusions

In this chapter we have studied the fiscal effects on the public sector from a life-cycle perspective. We have started with the net transfer structure over the life cycle and have used two methods, one more direct and one indirect, to remove costs for children from their parents' net transfer. From that, and from data on migration and

---

98   See Statistics Denmark (1999).

mortality, the total effects of the immigration of people of different ages have been calculated using different discount rates. The results are in line with those in the earlier chapters that are based on cross-sectional data. The immigrants from Western countries have mainly a positive financial effect on the public sector and non-Western immigrants a negative effect. The main factor behind the difference between the two groups is that the employment situation is very different. If the employment situation had been the same the net transfer difference would have been much smaller. This is shown by calculating the net transfer for the three groups – Danes, non-Western and Western immigrants – at the employment rates of 100 and zero. The total effects on public finance of immigration of a specific size, and with the actual age distribution at the time of immigration, have also been estimated. The results confirm the large differences between the two groups of immigrants and once more the large business-cycle dependence of the results.

In the analysis we have treated only the first generation of immigrants, i.e., we have not taken into consideration the transfers to and from the second generation. Information about the second-generation immigrants on the labour market is still scanty and therefore the pattern of what the net transfers will look like for this group is uncertain. This is partly due to insufficient information in identifying second-generation immigrants born before 1960, but more important is that immigration is a new phenomenon and therefore few children of immigrants have reached adulthood yet. The indications we have are that second generation immigrants will reach a higher employment rate than the first generation, but that it will still be lower than the Danes' employment rate.

Appendix Figures to Chapter 7

FIGURE 7.A1.

Net transfer to the public sector per person (three-year average; thousand Danish *kroner* in 1997 prices) in 1996, 1997 and 1998 for Danes, Western immigrants and non-Western immigrants. Net transfers to children under 18 are deducted from the net transfer to their parents. All

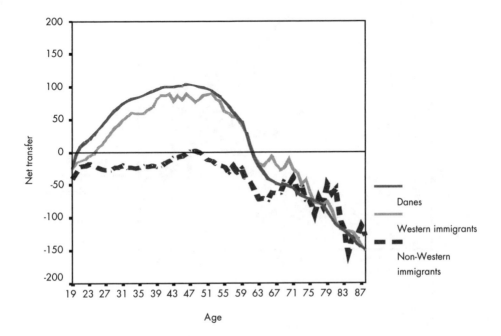

FIGURE 7.A2.

Net transfer to the public sector per person (three-year average; thousand Danish *kroner* in 1997 prices) in 1996, 1997 and 1998 for Danes, Western immigrants and non-Western immigrants. Net transfers to children under 18 are deducted from the net transfer to their parents. Men

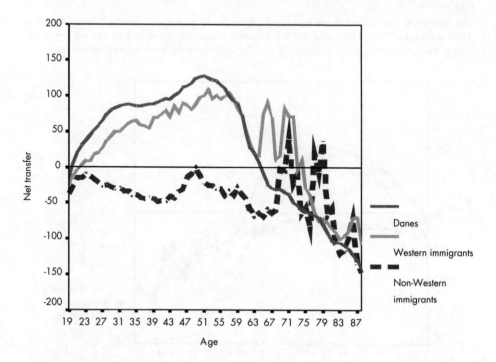

FIGURE 7.A3.

Net transfer to the public sector per person (three-year average; thousand Danish *kroner* in 1997 prices) in 1996, 1997 and 1998 for Danes, Western immigrants and non-Western immigrants. Net transfers to children under 18 are deducted from the net transfer to their parents. Women

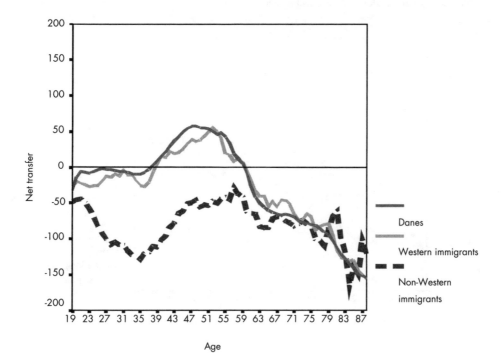

FIGURE 7.A4.

Net transfer to the public sector per person (three-year average; thousand Danish *kroner* in 1997 prices) in 1996, 1997 and 1998 for Danes, Western immigrants and non-Western immigrants for those with 100 as employment rate. Net transfers to children under 18 are deducted from the net transfer to their parents. All

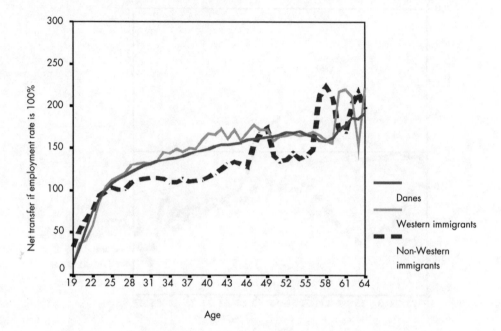

FIGURE 7.A5.

Net transfer to the public sector per person (three-year average; thousand Danish *kroner* in 1997 prices) in 1996, 1997 and 1998 for Danes, Western immigrants and non-Western immigrants for those with 100 as employment rate. Net transfers to children under 18 are deducted from the net transfer to their parents. Men

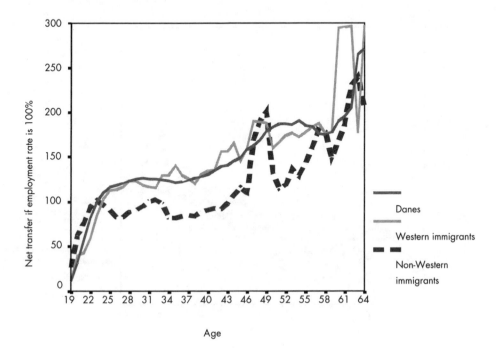

FIGURE 7.A6.

Net transfer to the public sector per person (three-year average; thousand Danish *kroner* in 1997 prices) in 1996, 1997 and 1998 for Danes, Western immigrants and non-Western immigrants for those with 100 as employment rate. Net transfers to children under 18 are deducted from the net transfer to their parents. Women

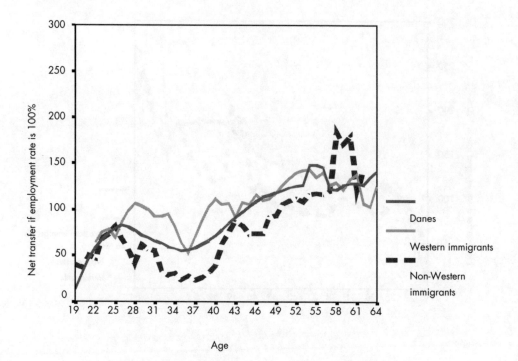

FIGURE 7.A7.

Net transfer to the public sector per person (three-year average; thousand Danish *kroner* in 1997 prices) in 1996, 1997 and 1998 for Danes, Western immigrants and non-Western immigrants for those with 0 as employment rate. Net transfers to children under 18 are deducted from the net transfer to their parents. All

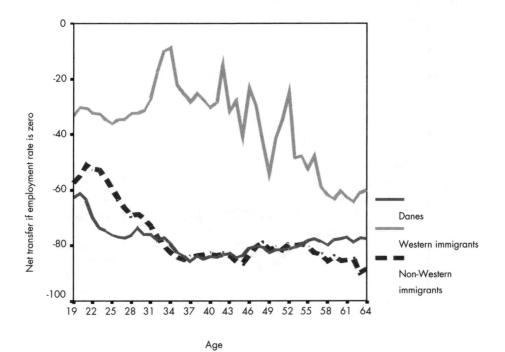

130   *Immigration and the Public Sector in Denmark*

FIGURE 7.A8.

Net transfer to the public sector per person (three-year average; thousand Danish *kroner* in 1997 prices) in 1996, 1997 and 1998 for Danes, Western immigrants and non-Western immigrants for those with 0 as employment rate. Net transfers to children under 18 are deducted from the net transfer to their parents. Men

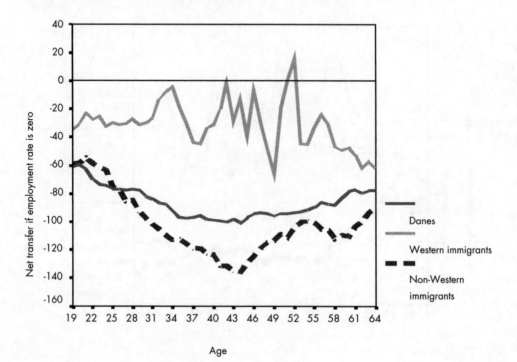

FIGURE 7.A9.

Net transfer to the public sector per person (three-year average; thousand Danish *kroner* in 1997 prices) in 1996, 1997 and 1998 for Danes, Western immigrants and non-Western immigrants for those with 0 as employment rate. Net transfers to children under 18 are deducted from the net transfer to their parents. Women

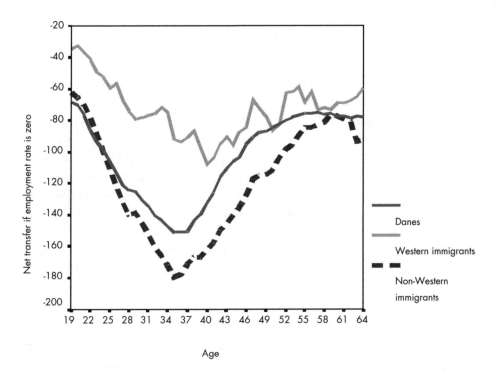

Age

Chapter 8

A Panel Data Study of the Development of the Individual Net Transfers

8.1 A panel data study

The studies of net transfers to the public sector in Denmark, which were presented in earlier chapters, have been based on cross-sectional data. In this chapter we will use panel data to study the factors that influence the net transfer to the public sector on the individual level. The study builds on a panel data set, the Law Model, for 1995 and 1998 of a 3.3 per cent sample of the population living in Denmark (Danes and immigrants).[99] With panel data it is possible to analyse if the individual net transfers to and from the public sector are stable over time or if there are large variations. It is also possible to validate the results we have received in the cross sectional studies.

When we made estimations in Chapter 6 on cross-sectional data, we drew conclusions from comparing people who have different employment rates and earnings, and the effects that changes in the same variables for one individual would have on his/her net transfer to the public sector. With panel data it is possible to study how changes in employment or in earnings influence the net transfers on the individual level. This does not mean, for example, that simply by relating changes in the employment rate to changes in the net transfer we can estimate the effect of the change in the employment rate. There are other changes – in age (everyone in the sample has become three years older between 1995 and 1998) and family status. The coefficients for the different variables in the equations determining the net transfer may also have changed due to growth in the economy, and due to changes in tax rates, transfer levels and the structure and costs of other public expenditure. If that is the case, then not only variables which represent changes in the variables have to be included, but also variables which represent the levels (the same variables as in the level equations).[100]

---

99 See Chapter 4 for a detailed presentation of the Law Model and the data used.
100 See the Appendix to this chapter.

8.2 Net transfers in 1995 and 1998

In Table 8.1 regression estimates for 1995 and 1998 are shown. The population consists of people aged 18 years and over. The net transfers to the children are not included in the transfers to their parents. The direct estimation method (see Chapter 7) is used. The results for 1998 in Table 8.1, columns (2) and (4), may be compared to the results in Table 6.1, columns (3) and (4), in which the net transfers to the children are included in the transfers to their parents. The values of the coefficients are almost the same, with the notable and expected exception, however, of two of the variables representing family status – 'unmarried with children' and 'married with children'.

The next step is to see if the two sets of coefficients for 1995 and 1998 differ from each other or not. To test this we have conducted Chow tests. The Chow test (which basically is an F test) is used to test for a structural change between two time periods, in this study the years 1995 and 1998. The null hypothesis is that there is structural stability between the two periods, i.e., that the function to be estimated has not undergone any structural change. An application of the Chow test on equations (1) and (2) in Table 8.1 rejects the null hypothesis on any conventional level and we draw the conclusion that there has been a structural change between 1995 and 1998. This means that the underlying functions of the estimated equations for the two years may be generated in different ways, and therefore differences between the equations should be interpreted with care. Applying the same test procedure on equations (3) and (4) generates the same result.

This does not mean that all coefficients have to be significantly different from each other in the 1995 and 1998 samples. However, in all but one case we found that the estimates of the coefficients from the two years were significantly different from each other. The exception is the variable representing earnings. The estimates of the coefficients for earnings in 1995 (in prices of 1998) and for earnings in 1998 are not significantly different from each other.[101]

Next we will compare the average transfer to the public sector for immigrants of different categories and for Danes in 1995 and 1998. Table 8.2 shows the numbers for all aged 18 years and over. For Danes and first-generation immigrants there is a change in the direction of more transfer to the public sector (or less transfer from the public sector) between 1995 and 1998. The changes are largest for those born in non-Western countries. The changes go in the other direction for some of the groups

---

101 This is not of course proof that they are equal. See Mayer (2001) for an illuminating discussion of what an acceptance of the null hypothesis (not significantly different) means.

TABLE 8.1.

Regression estimates (OLS) with net transfers to the public sector in 1995 (in 1998 prices) and 1998 in thousand Danish *kroner* as the dependent variable; and age, gender, family status, country of origin, employment rate and earnings as independent variables; all aged 18 and over

VARIABLES	1995	1998	1995	1998
	(1)	(2)	(3)	(4)
Constant	-157.792	-176.442	-111.708	-128.815
	(1.693)	(2.037)	(1.521)	(1.807)
Born in Denmark				
Both parents born in Denmark	0	0	0	0
One parent born in Denmark, one in a Western country	4.123	10.428	-0.734	-1.622
	(2.430)	(2.748)	(2.188)	(2.440)
One parent born in Denmark, one in a non-Western country	13.576	19.372	0.580	0.590
	(4.940)	(5.399)	(4.448)	(4.794)
Both parents born in a Western country	17.553	9.726	3.683	-2.394
	(6.021)	(6.949)	(5.421)	(5.428)
Both parents born in a non-Western country	5.998	26.966	-3.660	20.069
	(7.155)	(6.500)	(6.443)	(5.771)
Born outside Denmark				
Born in a Western country	17.903	23.870	7.576	10.401
	(1.753)	(1.997)	(1.577)	(1.771)
Born in a non-Western country	-10.677	-10.892	-21.921	-16.026
	(1.412)	(1.524)	(1.266)	(1.344)
Female	-27.119	-33.103	-16.194	-20.176
	(0.495)	(0.586)	(0.449)	(0.525)
Age	4.225	4.974	3.339	4.070
	(0.078)	(0.094)	(0.071)	(0.071)
Age^2	-0.042	-0.049	-0.039	-0.047
	(0.001)	(0.001)	(0.001)	(0.001)
Family status				
Unmarried, no children	0	0	0	0
Unmarried with children	-15.733	-11.191	-18.123	-13.794
	(1.533)	(0.834)	(1.380)	(1.634)
Married, no children	11.913	15.406	16.223	20.010
	(0.613)	(0.727)	(0.551)	(0.644)
Married with children	1.178	4.628	0.746	3.196
	(0.700)	(0.834)	(0.628)	(0.738)
Employment rate	1.889	2.058		
	(0.007)	(0.008)		
Earnings			0.698	0.701
			(0.002)	(0.002)
N	137,967	139,701	137,967	139,701
R^2(adj)	0.532	0.496	0.621	0.603

Note. Standard errors in parentheses. Only persons 18 years and older are included. Married stands for living together irrespective of whether a couple is formally married or not.

TABLE 8.2.

Average net transfers to the public sector in thousand Danish *kroner* in 1995 (amounts in 1998 prices in parentheses) and 1998; panel data; all aged 18 or over

	MEN		WOMEN	
	1995	1998	1995	1998
All	55.98 (59.64)	70.09	-5.05 (-5.38)	2.88
Born in Denmark				
Both parents born in Denmark	58.81 (62.66)	73.12	-3.43 (-3.66)	5.01
One parent born in Denmark, one in a Western country	60.44 (64.39)	81.49	4.45 (4.74)	17.67
One parent born in Denmark, one in a non-Western country	38.51 (41.03)	59.12	14.23 (15.16)	22.22
Both parents born in a Western country	46.46 (49.50)	64.99	18.88 (20.11)	1.30
Both parents born in a non-Western country	-8.69 (-9.25)	31.02	-41.29 (-43.99)	-19.35
Born outside Denmark				
Born in a Western country	64.85 (69.09)	79.33	-8.51 (-9.02)	-3.94
Born in a non-Western country	-24.63 (-26.24)	-5.07	-58.46 (-65.20)	-49.81

of second-generation immigrants. This may be explained by there being many young people in those groups, which means that many enter the group in a three year-period (reach the age of 18) and this leads to large changes in the age structure of the group. And as the transfers differ between age groups, these changes may have a large impact on the average net transfer to the public sector.

The average change in net transfer for the population aged 18 and over between 1995 and 1998 is enhanced to some extent by changes in the population. Those who are in the 1998 sample but not in the 1995 sample, have larger net transfers to the public sector than those who are in the 1995 but not in the 1998 sample. People who are in the population in 1995 but not in that of 1998 are those who have emigrated or died during that period. People who are in the population of 1998 and not in the 1995 population are those who have reached the age of 18 or have immigrated into the country during that period. See Table 8.3.

TABLE 8.3.

Average net transfers to the public sector in thousand Danish *kroner* in 1995 (amounts in 1998 prices in parentheses) or 1998 for those who were only included in one of the two years of the panel; all aged 18 or over in 1995 for exit, and all aged 18 and over in 1998 for entry

	MEN		WOMEN	
	1995	1998	1995	1998
Both types of exits				
Included in the 1995 sample but not in the 1998 sample, all	-50.63 (-53.94)		-104.47 (-111.30)	
Included in the 1995 sample but not in the 1998 sample, Danes	-56.39 (-60.07)		-109.37 (-116.52)	
Included in the 1995 sample but not in the 1998 sample, Western	33.42 (35.61)		-52.02 (-55.42)	
Included in the 1995 sample but not in the 1998 sample, non-Western	-29.82 (-31.73)		-57.86 (-61.64)	
Only emigrants				
Included in the 1995 sample but not in the 1998 sample, all	60.41 (64.36)		-3.97 (-4.23)	
Included in the 1995 sample but not in the 1998 sample, Danes	77.10 (82.15)		-0.52 (-0.56)	
Included in the 1995 sample but not in the 1998 sample, Western	35.93 (38.28)		-2.02 (-2.15)	
Included in the 1995 sample but not in the 1998 sample, non-Western	-10.03 (-10.69)		-39.94 (-42.55)	
Both types of entry				
Included in the 1998 sample but not in the 1995 sample, all		2.78		-27.16
Included in the 1998 sample but not in the 1995 sample, Danes		0.26		-25.75
Included in the 1998 sample but not in the 1995 sample, Western		67.85		-4.70
Included in the 1998 sample but not in the 1995 sample, non-Western		-16.34		-46.71
Only immigrants				
Included in the 1998 sample but not in the 1995 sample, all		52.63		-14.13
Included in the 1998 sample but not in the 1995 sample, Danes		93.12		7.30
Included in the 1998 sample but not in the 1995 sample, Western		72.50		-3.56
Included in the 1998 sample but not in the 1995 sample, non-Western		-9.23		-39.08

Of special interest is to compare the net transfers of those who have emigrated in the period with that of those who have immigrated.[102] Table 8.3 shows that the net transfer is about the same for those immigrating as for those emigrating. However, there are differences if we compare each group of men separately. The immigrants have a larger net transfer to the public sector than the emigrants. This paradox is due to a compositional effect. The non-Danish share is much larger among those immigrating than among those emigrating and the non-Danish group has lower net transfers on average.

To further study selectivity in emigration from Denmark we have made probit estimations of factors that influence the propensity to emigrate among those residing in Denmark in 1995.[103] We have made separate estimations for Danes, Western immigrants and non-Western immigrants. In all estimations age, gender and family status variables were included. Not unexpectedly, young, unmarried people without children emigrate more often in all three groups – Danes, Western and non-Western. Variables representing length of residence in Denmark (three categories and with the second generation as the comparison group) in the two probit estimations for immigrants, the coefficients of those variables are highly significant. Those who have resided for a short period in Denmark emigrate to a much higher extent (the effect is strongest for Western immigrants)[104]. If a variable representing net transfer to the public sector is included, the effect was significant and positive for the Danish group but not for the immigrants.

If the employment rate is included instead of the net transfer variable it is significant and negative for the Western immigrants on the 1 per cent level. But the value of the coefficient is small. The higher the employment rate the lower the propensity to emigrate. If a variable representing earnings is used instead of the employment rate, the coefficient for earnings is only significant (and positive) for the Danish group.

The effects of variables other than age and family status are small and the main conclusion from the probit estimates is that the emigration selection is mainly due to variables other than economic success or failure in Denmark. It means that the selection problem we have in the panel data studies when studying those who remain in Denmark for the whole period 1995-1998, and ignoring those who leave, is most likely of minor importance.

---

102 A problem with the comparison is that those who arrived in 1998 were only in Denmark part of the year. To control for that we have re-estimations excluding those who immigrated in 1998. The results change only to a small extent.

103 See Appendix 2 to this chapter for the results of the estimations.

104 One factor behind this result may be that quite a few of the Western immigrants come to Denmark to study and return after completing their studies.

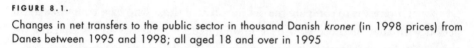

FIGURE 8.1.

Changes in net transfers to the public sector in thousand Danish *kroner* (in 1998 prices) from Danes between 1995 and 1998; all aged 18 and over in 1995

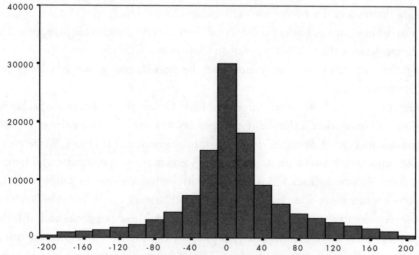

Note: mean = 6.82; standard deviation = 61.41, N = 116478 (only those changes between −200 and +200 are included)

8.3 Changes in net transfers to the public sector on the individual level

The numbers in Table 8.2 do not tell us if the changes are explained by a more or less uniform change for the individuals in each group or if there are larger variations within the groups. Therefore we will try to show in different ways how the net transfer changes on the individual level.

Figures 8.1-8.3 show that a small change is most common (-10 to +10 thousand Danish *kroner*) for Danes and Western immigrants as well as for non-Western immigrants, but also that the variations are large.[105] On the average the changes are positive for all three groups as indicated earlier by Table 8.3 and largest for the group of non-Western immigrants. The figures show that quite a few people have large changes, which is most likely explained by the fact that people pass between employment and non-employment (studies, unemployment, retirement). We will come back to a detailed analysis of the changes in section 8.4.

---

105 See Hansen et al. (1991) for a similar analysis of changes in disposable income using the Law Model.

FIGURE 8.2.

Changes in net transfers to the public sector in thousand Danish *kroner* (in 1998 prices) from Western immigrants between 1995 and 1998; all aged 18 and over in 1995

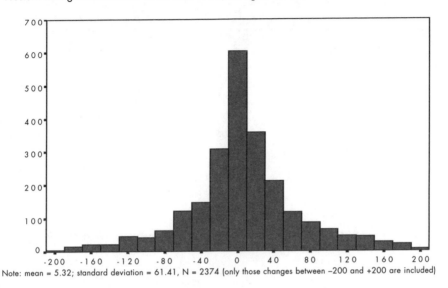

Note: mean = 5.32; standard deviation = 61.41, N = 2374 (only those changes between –200 and +200 are included)

FIGURE 8.3.

Changes in net transfers to the public sector in thousand Danish *kroner* (in 1998 prices) from non-Western immigrants between 1995 and 1998; all aged 18 and over in 1995

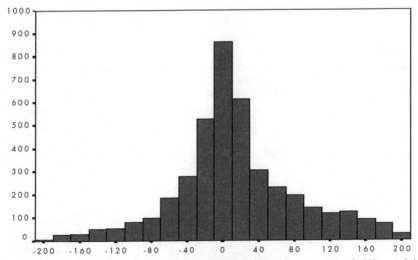

Note: mean = 29.87; standard deviation = 70.07, N = 4046 (only those changes between –200 and +200 are included)

TABLE 8.4A.

Changes in net transfers in thousand Danish *kroner* (in 1998 prices) between 1995 and 1998 (percentage distribution). Danes aged 18 and over

1995	1998					
	< -100	-100 – -50	-50 – +50	+50 – +100	> +100	ALL
< -100	5.4	2.4	0.9	0.4	0.3	9.4
-100 – -50	4.4	12.9	3.5	1.4	0.9	23.1
-50 – +50	1.0	3.9	8.5	4.4	3.3	21.0
+50 – +100	0.4	1.1	2.6	6.3	5.3	15.7
> +100	0.4	1.0	1.7	2.9	24.9	30.8
ALL	11.5	21.2	17.2	15.4	34.7	100.0

TABLE 8.4B.

Changes in net transfers in thousand Danish *kroner* (in 1998 prices) between 1995 and 1998 (percentage distribution). Western immigrants aged 18 and over

1995	1998					
	< -100	-100 – -50	-50 – +50	+50 – +100	> +100	ALL
< -100	6.4	2.4	1.0	0.2	0.4	10.3
-100– -50	4.1	11.1	3.4	0.8	0.8	20.2
-50– +50	1.3	4.9	13.7	4.0	3.5	27.4
+50– +100	0.4	0.8	2.1	5.4	4.6	13.4
> +100	0.4	0.9	2.0	2.7	22.6	28.6
ALL	12.5	20.2	22.3	13.1	32.0	100.0

TABLE 8.4C.

Changes in net transfers in thousand Danish *kroner* (in 1998 prices) between 1995 and 1998 (percentage distribution). Non-Western immigrants aged 18 and over

1995	1998					
	< -100	-100 – -50	-50 – +50	+50 – +100	> +100	ALL
< -100	10.9	6.7	3.6	1.0	0.7	22.8
-100 – -50	7.0	18.0	7.8	2.8	2.1	37.6
-50 – +50	2.3	6.2	9.3	3.3	2.4	23.5
+50 – +100	0.3	1.2	1.6	2.6	2.1	7.8
> +100	0.1	0.5	0.6	1.0	6.0	8.3
ALL	20.7	32.6	22.9	10.7	13.2	100.0

More of the pattern of change is shown in Table 8.4a-c. The three population groups are divided into five categories according to the size of the net transfer in 1995 and in 1998, respectively, and a mobility matrix is calculated for each group. It shows for example that many in the non-Western group who receive large net transfers in 1995 (100 thousand Danish *kroner* or more) receive less or are net contributors to the public sector in 1998.

Cross-sectional studies show that there is a systematic variation in net transfers over the life cycle – a net transfer from the public sector to children and young people, a net transfer from those of active age to the public sector, and a net transfer from the public sector to old people. We would expect to see a pattern mirroring that, if we study changes given the age. In Figure 8.4-8.6 the average change between 1995 and 1998 in net transfer to the public sector according to age (in 1995) is presented. We have also included those aged 17 and under in those figures.

The pattern is most evident for the Danish group in Figure 8.4. The change in net transfer is negative up to the age of eight years (in 1995, i.e. 11 years in 1998). This is mainly a result of the share in daycare increasing with age up to school starting age, and the schooling costs increasing at that level in the first years in school between 1995 and 1998. The changes in net transfer are small up to the age when most leave school when the change in the net transfer becomes strongly positive. The change of the net transfer is positive in almost all years up to the age of 55 (in 1995), which could be explained by increasing employment rates and higher wages in those

FIGURE 8.4.

Changes in net transfers to the public sector in thousand Danish *kroner* (in 1998 prices) between 1995 and 1998 according to age in 1995; Danes

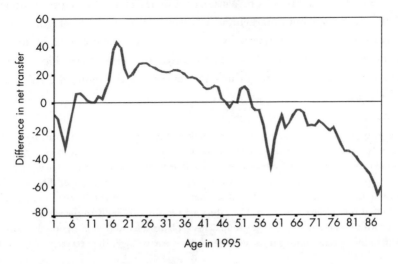

FIGURE 8.5.

Changes in net transfers to the public sector in thousand Danish *kroner* (in 1998 prices) between 1995 and 1998 according to age in 1995; Western immigrants

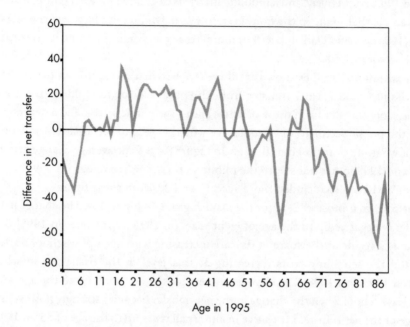

three years. The change in net transfer becomes strongly negative at the age when most leave the labour market.[106] It continues to be negative and increasingly so due to the costs of old age care increasing with age.

The pattern of change of net transfer to the public sector is more or less the same for the group of immigrants from Western countries as for the Danes; a top at the age of entry into the labour market and a dip at the age of exit. See Figure 8.5.

The pattern is different however in some respects for the group from non-Western countries compared with those for the other two groups. See Figure 8.6. For children and young people up to the age of entry it is the same, and the large in-

---

106 A contributing factor is that part of the expenditure for institutional old age care is distributed proportionally among all those aged 60 or more. The costs for old age care in the home are distributed among those who receive a pension with different values in three age groups (18-66, 67-79, 80-). The costs vary between the age groups due to that the share of those who have a pension varies and due to that the values that are set are different for the three age groups given that they receive a pension. The values are set proportionally to the average number of hours with home care in each age group. This explains the dip seen in figures for Danes and Western immigrants among those who were a few years younger than 60 years of age in 1995.

FIGURE 8.6.

Changes in net transfers to the public sector in thousand Danish *kroner* (in 1998 prices) between 1995 and 1998 according to age in 1995; non-Western immigrants

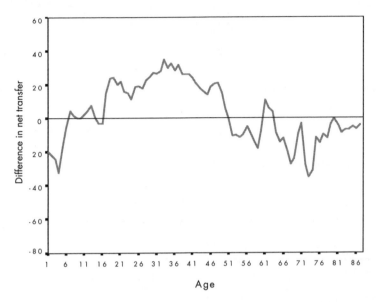

crease at the age of entry is also to be found. However, for those of active age up to 50 the increases between 1995 and 1998 are larger. This is probably to be explained by the fact that the improvement of the labour market situation in Denmark in those three years has been more important for non-Western immigrants than for Danes and Western immigrants. The difference is even greater for older people. It is difficult to explain this part of the pattern. However, as there are only a few older people from non-Western countries, it is difficult to draw any conclusions.

8.4 Changes in family status and in the employment rate

In the cross-sectional analysis we found that the net transfer to the public sector was strongly influenced by the individual employment rate and the family status[107]. We therefore expect that the net transfers to the public sector change as a result of change in the employment rate and of change in family status. Changes in employment status and family status are related to age, and the pattern we see in Figures 8.4-8.6 is probably determined by such changes to a large extent. In this section we

---

107 The effects of family status are lower in the estimates in this chapter than those in Chapter 6 as the net transfers for individuals independent of age are treated separately. In Chapter 6 the net transfers for those aged 17 and younger are added to those of their parents.

TABLE 8.5A.

Changes in family status between 1995 and 1998 (percentage distribution). Danes aged 18 and over

| | 1998 | | | | |
1995	FO	F1	F2	F3	ALL
F0 = single without children 17 years or younger	24.6	1.5	4.5	1.5	32.1
F1 = single with children 17 years or younger	1.2	1.5	0.2	0.6	3.5
F2 = married without children 17 years or younger	3.4	0.1	30.0	2.7	36.2
F3 = married with children 17 years or younger	3.9	0.9	3.8	19.6	28.2
ALL	33.1	4.0	38.5	24.4	100.0

Note: Married stands for living together irrespective of whether a couple is formally married or not.

TABLE 8.5B.

Changes in family status between 1995 and 1998 (percentage distribution). Western immigrants aged 18 and over

| | 1998 | | | | |
1995	FO	F1	F2	F3	ALL
F0 = single without children 17 years or younger	25.8	0.2	4.8	1.5	32.3
F1 = single with children 17 years or younger	1.2	1.5	0.2	0.6	3.5
F2 = married without children 17 years or younger	1.4	0.2	30.4	2.6	34.6
F3 = married with children 17 years or younger	3.9	1.1	3.6	21.0	29.6
ALL	32.3	3.0	39.0	25.7	100.0

Note: Married stands for living together irrespective of whether a couple is formally married or not.

TABLE 8.5C.

Changes in family status between 1995 and 1998 (percentage distribution). Non-Western immigrants aged 18 and over

| | 1998 | | | | |
1995	FO	F1	F2	F3	ALL
F0 = single without children 17 years or younger	19.7	0.3	4.7	3.0	27.7
F1 = single with children 17 years or younger	1.6	3.0	0.2	0.2	5.0
F2 = married without children 17 years or younger	2.5	0.3	12.5	3.6	18.9
F3 = married with children 17 years or younger	2.1	1.9	3.7	40.7	48.4
ALL	25.9	5.5	21.1	47.5	100.0

Note: Married stands for living together irrespective of whether a couple is formally married or not.

TABLE 8.6A.

Changes in employment rate between 1995 and 1998 (percentage distribution). Danes aged 18-62 in 1995

1995	1998				
	0	>0 – <50	50 – <98	98–100	ALL
0	11.8	2.4	1.8	1.5	17.5
>0 – <50	2.9	4.3	3.4	4.3	14.9
50 – <98	1.8	2.4	6.2	7.6	18.0
98–100	1.9	2.2	5.4	40.1	49.6
ALL	18.4	11.3	16.8	53.5	100.0

TABLE 8.6B.

Changes in employment rate between 1995 and 1998 (percentage distribution). Western immigrants aged 18-62 in 1995

1995	1998				
	0	>0 – <50	50 – <98	98–100	ALL
0	19.4	4.1	2.6	2.0	28.1
>0 – <50	4.5	3.8	2.9	3.2	14.4
50 – <98	1.6	2.6	6.1	6.7	17.0
98–100	1.7	2.3	4.5	32.0	40.5
ALL	27.2	12.8	16.1	43.9	100.0

TABLE 8.6C.

Changes in employment rate between 1995 and 1998 (percentage distribution). Non-Western immigrants aged 18-62 in 1995

1995	1998				
	0	>0 – <50	50 – <98	98–100	ALL
0	38.8	7.6	6.9	4.4	57.7
>0 – <50	5.5	4.5	3.5	2.9	16.4
50 – <98	2.6	2.5	4.0	2.9	12.0
98–100	1.1	1.3	2.6	8.9	13.9
ALL	48.0	15.9	17.0	19.1	100.0

will give some information of the changes in family status and employment rate between the two years before turning to results from regression estimates.

Tables 8.5a-c show that approximately 25 per cent of those aged 18 and over change family status in a three-year period. It is also evident that some types of change in family status are frequent and others infrequent (leading to problems in estimating the consequences of such changes).

Tables 8.6a-c show the corresponding changes in the employment rate divided into four categories.[108] Only those of active age (18-62 years of age in 1995) are included in those tables. Close to 45 per cent of non-Western immigrants have changed employment category between 1995 and 1998. For Western immigrants and Danes the corresponding figure is lower, 39 and 38 per cent respectively. Only 9 per cent of the non-Western immigrants are employed full-time both in 1995 and in 1998 compared to 40 per cent of the Danes and 32 per cent of the Western immigrants.

Note that only those of active age are included, if all aged 18 and over are included the mobility will be lower as most older people have a stable employment rate of zero per cent. As well as the changes between the categories shown here there are of course changes within two of the categories (>0 – <50 and 50 – <98).

8.5 A regression analysis of individual changes in net transfer to the public sector

The next step of the analysis is to estimate a regression equation with net transfer to the public sector as the dependent variable. The explanatory variables are change in family status, country of origin, gender and age and age^2 and one of two alternatives: 1) change in the employment rate and the employment rate in 1995, or 2) change in earnings.[109] The family status variables are condensed to four to avoid alternatives with very few observations.

The estimates with the employment rate alternative are shown in Table 8.7 for all, and separately for men and women. As expected, the coefficient for the change of the employment rate is highly significant but it is somewhat lower than expected from the cross-section estimates. We will come back to that question in Section 8.6. The coefficient for the variable representing the employment rate is 0.164, which is close

---

108 The full employment level is set to 98 per cent, due to the method for calculation of the employment rate in the Law Model having been changed from 1997 on. See Chapter 4 for details.

109 See the Appendix to this chapter and Section 8.1 for the motivation for the selection of the variables included in the estimations.

TABLE 8.7.

Regression estimates (OLS) with the change in net transfer to the public sector (in thousand Danish *kroner*, 1998 prices) between 1995 and 1998 as the dependent variable; and country of origin, age, gender, change in employment rate, employment rate in 1995 and change in family status as independent variables

VARIABLES	ALL	MEN	WOMEN
Constant	-8.254 (1.876)	6.483 (3.463)	-19.948 (2.027)
Born in Denmark			
Both parents born in Denmark	0	0	0
One parent born in Denmark, one in a Western country	-7.150 (1.813)	8.449 (2.757)	5.629 (2.230)
One parent born in Denmark, one in a non-Western country	7.090 (3.740)	6.223 (6.213)	9.747 (3.993)
Both parents born in a Western country	-8.150 (7.514)	2.032 (9.806)	-20.802 (11.442)
Both parents born in a non-Western country	32.739 (26.990)	40.821 (47.567)	21.387 (6.059)
Born outside Denmark			
Born in a Western country	-0.919 (2.108)	-0.870 (3.992)	-0.959 (1.873)
Born in a non-Western country	0.368 (1.074)	3.752 (1.804)	3.101 (1.117)
Female	-3.314 (0.541)		
Age in 1995	0.768 (0.089)	-0.182 (0.157)	1.364 (0.100)
(Age in 1995)^2	-0.012 (0.001)	-0.002 (0.002)	-0.019 (0.001)
Change in employment rate	1.754 (0.010)	1.884 (0.019)	1.627 (0.009)
Employment rate in 1995	0.164 (0.008)	0.230 (0.015)	0.108 (0.007)
Change in family status			
No change	0	0	0
From single to married	0.395 (0.767)	-1.011 (1.232)	-0.897 (0.885)
From married to single	-6.804 (1.770)	-13.886 (3.895)	-1.189 (1.216)
From not parent to parent	-17.637 (0.909)	-3.144 (1.307)	-36.403 (1.200)
From parent to not parent	-0.802 (1.079)	-1.185 (2.066)	1.605 (1.100)
N	130,333	63,692	66,641
R^2(adj)	0.231	0.166	0.404

Notes. Standard errors in parentheses. Individuals 18 years and older in 1995 are included. Parent = parent with children in the household who are 17 years or younger. Not parent = the individual has no children in the household who are 17 years or younger. Married stands for living together irrespective of whether a couple is formally married or not. The employment rate varies between 0 and 100.

to the difference between the two coefficients in the cross-section analysis: 2.058 – 1.889 = 0.169.[110]

The coefficient for the transition from being married to being single is significantly negative for men but not for women. The coefficients are significantly negative for men and for women who go from childlessness to becoming a parent. Being a parent is defined here as being parent to a child who is 17 years or younger. The coefficient for the transition from being a parent to being childless according to this definition, which in the large majority of cases means that the child is 17 years or younger in 1995 and in 1998 has become 18 years or older, is not significant.

The female variable is significant and the size of the coefficient is in accordance with what we could expect from the cross-section estimates. In most cases the values of the nationality group variables are in accordance with what we could expect from the cross-section estimates. They are insignificant in most cases, however.

The age variables are significant in the estimation in which all individuals are included, and the values of the coefficients are in accordance with what we should expect from the cross-section estimates and the relation between the coefficients shown in the Appendix to this chapter. However, the estimates for men and women separately are not as expected. The coefficients for age and age squared are not significant in the equation for men, but they are significant and too large compared to what we should expect from the cross section estimates in the equation for women.[111] If only age – and not age squared – is included in the estimation of the equation for men, the coefficient becomes highly significant. It is possible that the effect of age on the net transfer to the public sector is represented in a too simple way.

In Table 8.8 the corresponding regression estimates with change in earnings instead of change in the employment rate and the employment rate in 1995 are shown. The variable for earnings in 1995 is not included, as the coefficients for 1995 and 1998 in the cross-section estimates are not significantly different from each other.[112] The coefficient for earnings is highly significant but somewhat lower than the estimate from the cross-section regression. See section 8.6 for a comparison.

Most of the variables have values similar to the estimates with the employment variables included that are shown in Table 8.7. The coefficients for the age variables, which are significant, have larger values than what we could expect from the cross-section estimates.

---

110 See the Appendix to this chapter.

111 The cross-section estimations for men and women separately are not shown in this chapter.

112 In a test where we added earnings in 1995 to the explanatory variables, the coefficient for that variable was small and not significant.

TABLE 8.8.

Regression estimates (OLS) with the change in net transfer to the public sector (in thousand Danish *kroner*, 1998 prices) between 1995 and 1998 as the dependent variable; and country of origin, age, gender, change in earnings and change in family status as independent variables

VARIABLES	ALL	MEN	WOMEN
Constant	-17.005 (4.147)	-4.282 (7.593)	-31.461 (1.952)
Born in Denmark			
Both parents born in Denmark	0	0	0
One parent born in Denmark, one in a Western country	3.712 (1.733)	4.876 (2.743)	2.440 (1.843)
One parent born in Denmark, one in a non-Western country	0.340 (2.733)	0.361 (4.427)	1.471 (3.145)
Both parents born in a Western country	-6.035 (6.386)	3.757 (8.661)	-14.223 (9.491)
Both parents born in a non-Western country	40.779 (27.916)	55.411 (49.098)	21.233 (6.004)
Born outside Denmark			
Born in a Western country	1.296 (1.842)	3.340 (3.438)	-0.487 (1.738)
Born in a non-Western country	2.046 (0.920)	4.764 (1.553)	-0.747 (0.998)
Female	-2.837 (0.578)		
Age in 1995	1.462 (0.166)	0.929 (0.307)	1.879 (0.090)
(Age in 1995)^2	-0.020 (0.001)	-0.015 (0.003)	-0.023 (0.001)
Change in earnings	0.670 (0.029)	0.600 (0.043)	0.803 (0.007)
Change in family status			
No change	0	0	0
From single to married	0.268 (0.644)	-1.067 (1.038)	-1.255 (0.718)
From married to single	-9.507 (1.747)	-16.760 (3.860)	-4.422 (1.153)
From not parent to parent	-20.088 (0.901)	-2.211 (1.109)	-35.560 (1.073)
From parent to not parent	1.386 (1.006)	2.321 (1.969)	2.705 (1.008)
N	130,333	63,692	66,641
R^2(adj)	0.270	0.200	0.473

Notes. Standard errors in parentheses. Individuals 18 years and older in 1995 are included. Parent = parent with children in the household who are 17 years or younger. Not parent = the individual has no children in the household who are 17 years or younger. Married stands for living together irrespective of whether a couple is formally married or not. The employment rate varies between 0 and 100.

TABLE 8.9.

Regression estimates (OLS) with the change in net transfer to the public sector (in thousand Danish *kroner*, 1998 prices) between 1995 and 1998 as the dependent variable; and age, change in employment rate, employment rate in 1995 and change in family status as independent variables. Men

VARIABLES	DANES	WESTERN IMMIGRANTS	NON-WESTERN IMMIGRANTS
Constant	8.617 (3.489)	-16.659 (28.592)	-4.423 (19.330)
Age in 1995	-0.219 (0.162)	0.216 (1.380)	-0.361 (1.408)
(Age in 1995)^2	-0.002 (0.002)	-0.001 (0.014)	0.011 (0.021)
Change in employment rate	1.879 (0.020)	2.050 (0.191)	1.933 (0.102)
Employment rate in 1995	0.222 (0.016)	0.249 (0.107)	0.310 (0.106)
Change in family status			
No change	0	0	0
From single to married	-0.680 (1.271)	-8.099 (7.424)	-4.823 (8.342)
From married to single	-13.966 (4.199)	-16.501 (11.809)	-13.316 (6.115)
From not parent to parent	-3.152 (1.380)	7.478 (9.192)	-4.804 (6.412)
From parent to not parent	-1.788 (2.165)	8.489 (15.196)	4.846 (5.197)
N	59,432	1,176	2,229
R^2(adj)	0.159	0.211	0.315

Notes. Standard errors in parentheses. Individuals 18 years and older in 1995 are included. Parent = parent with children in the household who are 17 years or younger. Not parent = the individual has no children in the household who are 17 years or younger. Married stands for living together irrespective of whether a couple is formally married or not. The employment rate varies between 0 and 100.

The results could differ between Danes and the two groups of immigrants. Therefore, regressions for each nationality group and gender are estimated. In Table 8.9 and 8.10 the results for the alternative with change in the employment rate and the employment rate in 1995 are shown. The results are mainly the same as in Table 8.7. The coefficients for the employment rate variables are larger for men than for women in each group. The family status change variables also differ between men and women for each group. The effect on net transfer from becoming a parent is much larger for women than for men for all three groups.

TABLE 8.10.

Regression estimates (OLS) with the change in net transfer to the public sector (in thousand Danish *kroner*, 1998 prices) between 1995 and 1998 as the dependent variable; and age, change in employment rate, employment rate in 1995 and change in family status as independent variables. Women

VARIABLES	DANES	WESTERN IMMIGRANTS	NON-WESTERN IMMIGRANTS
Constant	-18.924 (2.106)	-31.211 (16.299)	-26.630 (7.944)
Age in 1995	1.341 (0.104)	1.629 (0.734)	1.296 (0.395)
(Age in 1995)^2	-0.019 (0.001)	-0.020 (0.008)	-0.015 (0.005)
Change in employment rate	1.628 (0.009)	1.641 (0.086)	1.574 (0.033)
Employment rate in 1995	0.105 (0.008)	0.091 (0.044)	-1.172 (0.034)
Change in family status			
No change	0	0	0
From single to married	-1.386 (0.924)	-4.470 (6.500)	9.724 (4.231)
From married to single	-1.254 (1.269)	3.609 (11.491)	-11.448 (4.745)
From not parent to parent	-36.639 (1.275)	-40.492 (9.209)	-32.034 (4.203)
From parent to not parent	0.843 (1.146)	15.787 (6.331)	13.340 (4.552)
N	62,509	1,328	2,044
R^2(adj)	0.398	0.348	0.604

Notes. Standard errors in parentheses. Individuals 18 years and older in 1995 are included. Parent = parent with children in the household who are 17 years or younger. Not parent = the individual has no children in the household who are 17 years or younger. Married stands for living together irrespective of whether a couple is formally married or not. The employment rate varies between 0 and 100.

The coefficients for the age variables for men from the three groups are not significantly different from zero.

In Table 8.11 and 8.12 the results for the alternative with change in earnings is shown. The results are mainly the same as in Table 8.8. The coefficient for the earnings variable is larger for women than for men in each group. The coefficients of family status change variables also differ between the groups and between men and women. The estimates for the age variables for men from Western countries and non-Western countries are not significantly different from zero.

TABLE 8.11.

Regression estimates (OLS) with the change in net transfer to the public sector (in thousand Danish *kroner*, 1998 prices) between 1995 and 1998 as the dependent variable; and age, change in earnings and change in family status as independent variables. Men

VARIABLES	DANES	WESTERN IMMIGRANTS	NON-WESTERN IMMIGRANTS
Constant	-2.449 (8.302)	-7.838 (20.541)	16.685 (21.044)
Age in 1995	0.877 (0.333)	0.658 (0.928)	-0.645 (1.298)
(Age in 1995)^2	-0.015 (0.003)	-0.007 (0.009)	0.012 (0.019)
Change in earnings	0.590 (0.047)	0.687 (0.051)	0.742 (0.022)
Change in family status			
No change	0	0	0
From single to married	-0.733 (1.103)	-1.219 (6.222)	-4.298 (3.636)
From married to single	-17.108 (4.163)	-18.774 (10.839)	-9.855 (5.596)
From not parent to parent	-1.353 (1.185)	-6.366 (6.251)	-8.378 (3.756)
From parent to not parent	1.602 (2.070)	19.535 (14.258)	6.695 (5.786)
N	59,432	1,176	2,229
R^2(adj)	0.187	0.429	0.367

Notes. Standard errors in parentheses. Individuals 18 years and older in 1995 are included. Parent = parent with children in the household who are 17 years or younger. Not parent = the individual has no children in the household who are 17 years or younger. Married stands for living together irrespective of whether a couple is formally married or not. The employment rate varies between 0 and 100.

That the coefficient for the change in earnings is higher for women than for men in all three nationality groups is probably explained by women having lower earnings than men. Therefore the marginal net transfer rate is highest for those with low earnings due to income-tested transfer payments (a part of a poverty trap). Thus people with lower earnings contribute more to the public sector for each extra *krone* earned.

TABLE 8.12.

Regression estimates (OLS) with the change in net transfer to the public sector between 1995 and 1998 (in thousand Danish *kroner*, 1998 prices) as the dependent variable; and age, change in earnings and change in family status as independent variables. Women

VARIABLES	DANES	WESTERN IMMIGRANTS	NON-WESTERN IMMIGRANTS
Constant	-30.703 (2.038)	-42.790 (14.984)	-29.432 (7.442)
Age in 1995	1.858 (0.094)	2.121 (0.657)	1.521 (0.371)
(Age in 1995)^2	-0.023 (0.001)	-0.025 (0.007)	-0.017 (0.004)
Change in earnings	0.802 (0.008)	0.775 (0.025)	0.852 (0.014)
Change in family status			
No change	0	0	0
From single to married	-1.857 (0.750)	4.381 (3.806)	7,522 (4.138)
From married to single	-4.501 (1.204)	6.515 (11.856)	-13.496 (4.151)
From not parent to parent	-35.379 (1.140)	-40.928 (7.115)	-34.721 (4.644)
From parent to not parent	2.053 (1.049)	14.583 (6.779)	12.946 (3.909)
N	62,509	1,328	2,044
R^2(adj)	0.465	0.460	0.656

Notes. Standard errors in parentheses. Individuals 18 years and older in 1995 are included. Parent = parent with children in the household who are 17 years or younger. Not parent = the individual has no children in the household who are 17 years or younger. Married stands for living together irrespective of whether a couple is formally married or not. The employment rate varies between 0 and 100.

8.6 A comparison of cross-section and panel estimates

In Table 8.13 the values for cross-section estimates and panel estimates on the two central variables employment/change in employment, and earnings/change in earnings are presented.

The cross-section estimates of the employment variables for the various groups show a variation of the coefficient estimates between 1.620 (non-Western women) to 2.308 (Danish men). According to these estimates a change from zero to full employ-

TABLE 8.13.

Estimates of effects of employment and earnings on net transfers to the public sector according to cross-section (1998) and panel estimates

GROUP, VARIABLE	CROSS-SECTION	PANEL
ALL, MEN AND WOMEN		
Employment/ change in employment (panel)	2.058 (0.008) ***	1.754 (0.010) ***
Earnings/ change in earnings (panel)	0.701 (0.002)	0.670 (0.029)
ALL, MEN		
Employment/ change in employment (panel)	2.279 (0.015) ***	1.884 (0.020) ***
Earnings/ change in earnings (panel)	0.674 (0.009)	0.600 (0.043)
ALL, WOMEN		
Employment/ change in employment (panel)	1.827 (0.007) ***	1.627 (0.009) ***
Earnings/ change in earnings (panel)	0.746 (0.003) ***	0.803 (0.007) ***
DANES, MEN AND WOMEN		
Employment/ change in employment (panel)	2.076 (0.008) ***	1.750 (0.011) ***
Earnings/ change in earnings (panel)	0.700 (0.007)	0.664 (0.031)
DANES, MEN		
Employment/ change in employment (panel)	2.308 (0.014)***	1.879 (0.020) ***
Earnings/ change in earnings (panel)	0.672 (0.010)	0.590 (0.047)
DANES, WOMEN		
Employment/ change in employment (panel)	1.838 (0.007) ***	1.628 (0.009) ***
Earnings/ change in earnings (panel)	0.747 (0.003) ***	0.802 (0.008) ***
WESTERN, MEN AND WOMEN		
Employment/ change in employment (panel)	1.756 (0.063)	1.865 (0.108)
Earnings/ change in earnings (panel)	0.648 (0.023)	0.709 (0.036)
WESTERN, MEN		
Employment/ change in employment (panel)	1.738 (0.112)	2.050 (0.191)
Earnings/ change in earnings (panel)	0.692 (0.027)	0.687 (0.051)

TABLE 8.13. (continued)

GROUP, VARIABLE	CROSS-SECTION	PANEL
WESTERN, WOMEN		
Employment/ change in employment (panel)	1.749 (0.057)	1.641 (0.086)
Earnings/ change in earnings (panel)	0.634 (0.027) ***	0.775 (0.025) ***
NON-WESTERN, MEN AND WOMEN		
Employment/ change in employment (panel)	1.876 (0.048)	1.779 (0.056)
Earnings/ change in earnings (panel)	0.764 (0.010)	0.770 (0.018)
NON-WESTERN, MEN		
Employment/ change in employment (panel)	2.069 (0.087)	1.933 (0.103)
Earnings/ change in earnings (panel)	0.763 (0.012)	0.742 (0.022)
NON-WESTERN, WOMEN		
Employment/ change in employment (panel)	1.620 (0.030)	1.574 (0.033)
Earnings/ change in earnings (panel)	0.756 (0.017) ***	0.852 (0.014) ***

*** = significant difference between the cross-section and panel estimates on the 1 per cent level; ** = significant difference on the 5 per cent level; * = significant difference on the 10 per cent level.

ment for an individual means an increase in the net transfer to the public sector in the interval from 162,000 to 230,800 Danish *kroner*. The panel estimates vary less between the groups. The interval is between 155,100 (non-Western women) to 205,000 Danish *kroner* (Western men). In ten out of the twelve cases the cross-section estimate is higher than the panel estimate. In six of the cases the difference between the coefficients is significant on the 1 per cent level. In two cases (Western men and women, and Western men) the panel estimate is higher than the cross-section estimate. The difference is not significantly different from zero at the 1 per cent level in either of those cases.

Even if there are significant differences the main impression is that the cross-section estimates used in earlier chapters are not very far away from panel data estimates shown here, albeit giving higher estimates. The explanation for the difference is most likely that when we compare different people with different employment rates as in the cross-section studies, they probably also differ in other respects. For example, those with a (constant) high employment rate have a higher wage rate than those with an increase in the employment rate between 1995 and 1998. They are therefore receiving less in transfer payments and paying more in taxes taking other variables into account at a given employment rate. We see that by comparing the wage rates for groups with different employment histories. The average hourly wage rate in 1998 for those with full employment in both 1995 and 1998 was 165.15 Danish *kroner*. The average wage rate in 1998 for those who were employed full time and full year in 1998 but not in 1995 was considerably lower. Of those not employed in 1995 but who worked full time in 1998 the wage rate was 100.22 Danish *kroner* in 1998; for those employed 1-10 per cent in 1995 and full time in 1998, 122.43 Danish *kroner*; for those employed 11-50 per cent in 1995 and full time in 1998, 127.21 Danish *kroner*; and for those employed 51-97 per cent in 1995 and full time in 1998, 137.16 Danish *kroner*. Those with full employment in both years have relatively high hourly wage rates, compared to those with low employment one or both of the years. This pattern is clear for the Danish group but less so for the two groups of immigrants.

The cross-section estimates of the earnings variables for the different groups show a variation of coefficient estimates between 0.634 (Western women) to 0.764 (non-Western men and women). According to these estimates an increase of earnings by 100,000 Danish *kroner* led to an increase in the net transfer to the public sector in the interval from 63,400 to 76,400 Danish *kroner*. The panel estimates vary somewhat more between the groups. The interval is between 0.590 (Danish men) to 0.873 (non-Western women). In six out of the twelve estimates the cross-section estimate is higher than the panel estimate. The difference is not significant on the 1 per cent level in any of the cases. In six of the estimations the panel estimates are higher than the cross-section ones. In four of these cases the difference is significantly different from zero at the 1 per cent level. These cases are the four groups with only women. The explanation may be that women are more often in an earnings bracket with high marginal effects and also that the marginal effect has increased between 1995 and 1998 in that interval. To test that we have made separate estimates for those in four different earnings intervals: 0-100, 101-200, 201-300 and 301-. Compared to men, women are overrepresented in the earnings interval 101-200. The coefficients in 1995 for women are in the four intervals 0.771, 0.789, 0.687 and 0.644, respectively. In 1998 the corresponding estimates are 0.755, 0.809, 0.651 and 0.731. The marginal rate is highest in the interval 101-200 and the value of the coefficient is higher in 1998 and in 1995. The results support the hypothesis.

8.7 Conclusions

In the study presented in this chapter it has been possible for the first time to use panel data on net transfers to the public sector from immigrants in Denmark. One finding is that during the three-year period from 1995 to 1998 there are great changes on the individual level in net transfers to the public sector. Some of those changes are due to young people entering the labour market and older people leaving the labour market, but there are also large changes connected to those of active age.

The most important factor behind changes in net transfers is the change in the individual's employment rate and earnings. This confirms and strengthens the results from the cross-section studies. If a person goes from not being employed to full employment this means a strengthening of the public finance by an amount of 150 to 200 thousand Danish *kroner*. The marginal net transfer rate for earnings is close to 70 per cent for the total population and even higher for the non-Western immigrants.

The results show that attempts to increase the employment rate and thereby earnings for immigrants may have very large positive effects for the public sector. The employment rate for the non-Western immigrants has increased but it is still much lower for them than for other groups. Policies that are efficient in improving the employment situation of the non-Western immigrants are therefore in great demand.

Appendix 1 to Chapter 8.

Parameters estimated in the equations with change in net transfer as dependent variable

Case 1. Variables which are included in linear form in the level equation and which change between 1995 and 1998 (employment rate; earnings)

$$b_{98}E_{98} - b_{95}E_{95} = b_{98}(E_{95}+\Delta E) - b_{95}E_{95} = b_{98}\Delta E + (b_{98}-b_{95})E_{95}$$

If the coefficient changes between 1995 and 1998, both the change in the variable and the level in 1995 should be included; if the coefficient is the same in 1995 and 1998 only the change of the variable should be included.

Case 2. Variables which are included in linear form in the level equation and which do not change between 1995 and 1998 (country of origin, female)

$$b_{98}F - b_{95}F = (b_{98} - b_{95})F$$

The variable should be included only if the coefficient changes between 1995 and 1998.

Case 3. The variable representing age – linear and quadratic terms – and which changes by 3 between 1995 and 1998 (all by becoming 3 years older)

$$a_{98}Age_{98} + b_{98}Age_{98}^2 - a_{95}Age_{95} - b_{95}Age_{95}^2 =$$
$$a_{98}(Age_{95}+3) + b_{98}(Age_{95}+3)^2 - a_{95}Age_{95} - b_{95}Age_{95}^2 =$$
$$(a_{98}-a_{95})Age_{95} + 3a_{98} + 9b_{98} + 6b_{98}Age_{95} + b_{98}Age_{95}^2 - b_{95}Age_{95}^2 =$$
$$(3a_{98}+9b_{98}) + [(a_{98}-a_{95})+6b_{98}]Age_{95} + (b_{98}-b_{95})Age_{95}^2$$

Appendix 2 to Chapter 8.

Probit estimates of the propensity to emigrate from Denmark

TABLE 8.A1.

Probit estimates (marginal effects) for 1995. The dependent variable takes the value one if the individual has moved from Denmark during the time period 1996-1998. Age, gender, family status, country of origin, length of stay in Denmark, employment rate, earnings and net transfers (both earnings and net transfers are measured in ten thousand Danish *kroner*) as the independent variables. All

VARIABLES	(1)	(2)	(3)
Born in Denmark			
Both parents born in Denmark	0	0	0
One parent born in Denmark, one in a Western country	0.001 (0.002)	0.002 (0.002)	0.002 (0.002)
One parent born in Denmark, one in a non-Western country	0.009 (0.005)	0.010 (0.005)	0.010 (0.005)
Both parents born in a Western country	0.023 (0.011)	0.025 (0.011)	0.025 (0.011)
Both parents born in non-Western country	0.0005 (0.0040)	0.002 (0.005)	0.002 (0.005)
Born outside Denmark			
Born in a Western country			
Immigrated >7 years	0.067 (0.020)	0.068 (0.020)	0.067 (0.020)
Immigrated 3-7	0.102 (0.019)	0.113 (0.020)	0.111 (0.020)
Immigrated <1-3	0.245 (0.020)	0.270 (0.020)	0.267 (0.020)
Born in a non-Western country			
Immigrated >7 years	0.003 (0.003)	0.006 (0.004)	0.006 (0.004)
Immigrated 3-7	0.007 (0.003)	0.012 (0.004)	0.013 (0.004)
Immigrated <1-3	0.027 (0.005)	0.041 (0.006)	0.044 (0.007)
Female	-0.00010 (0.00042)	-0.00005 (0.00042)	0.00008 (0.00042)
Age	-0.0004 (0.0001)	-0.0004 (0.0001)	-0.0004 (0.0001)

TABLE 8.A1. (continued)

VARIABLES	(1)	(2)	(3)
Family status			
Unmarried, no children	0	0	0
Unmarried with children	-0.003 (0.0008)	-0.003 (0.0007)	-0.003 (0.0007)
Married, no children	-0.003 (0.0005)	-0.004 (0.0005)	-0.004 (0.0005)
Married with children	-0.004 (0.0004)	-0.005 (0.0004)	-0.005 (0.0004)
Employment rate	-0.00005 (0.000005)		
Earnings		0.00005 (0.00002)	
Net transfer			0.00008 (0.00002)
N	116,582	116,582	116,582
Likelihood ratio	2598.51	2517.35	2526.66

Note. Standard errors in parentheses (note that probit estimations are based on the normal distribution). Only persons 18 years and older are included. Married stands for living together irrespective of whether a couple is formally married or not.

TABLE 8.A2.

Probit estimates (marginal effects) for 1995. The dependent variable takes the value one if the individual has moved from Denmark during the time period 1996-1998. Age, gender, family status, country of origin, length of stay in Denmark, employment rate, earnings and net transfers (both earnings and net transfers are measured in ten thousand Danish kroner) as independent variables. Danes

VARIABLES	(1)	(2)	(3)
Female	-0.0007 (0.0004)	0.0003 (0.0004)	0.0004 (0.0004)
Age	-0.0004 (0.0001)	-0.0004 (0.0001)	-0.0004 (0.0001)
Family status			
Unmarried, no children	0	0	0
Unmarried with children	-0.003 (0.001)	-0.003 (0.006)	-0.003 (0.006)
Married, no children	-0.002 (0.005)	-0.003 (0.005)	-0.003 (0.004)
Married with children	-0.003 (0.004)	-0.004 (0.004)	-0.004 (0.004)
Employment rate	-0.00004 (0.000005)		
Earnings		0.00005 (0.00002)	
Net transfer			0.00008 (0.00002)
N	108,382	108,382	108,382
Likelihood ratio	1232.18	1164.76	1172.29

Note. Standard errors in parentheses (note that probit estimations are based on the normal distribution). Only persons 18 years and older are included. Married stands for living together irrespective of whether a couple is formally married or not.

TABLE 8.A3.

Probit estimates (marginal effects) for 1995. The dependent variable takes the value one if the individual has moved from Denmark during the time period 1996-1998. Age, gender, family status, country of origin, length of stay in Denmark, employment rate, earnings and net transfer (both earnings and net transfers measured in ten thousand Danish *kroner*) as independent variables. Western immigrants

VARIABLES	(1)	(2)	(3)
Born in Denmark (second generation)	0	0	0
Immigrated >7 years	0.107 (0.035)	0.109 (0.036)	0.110 (0.036)
Immigrated 3-7	0.149 (0.032)	0.163 (0.033)	0.166 (0.033)
Immigrated <1-3	0.285 (0.031)	0.310 (0.032)	0.316 (0.032)
Female	-0.005 (0.008)	-0.002 (0.008)	-0.0008 (0.0081)
Age	-0.0015 (0.0003)	-0.0014 (0.0003)	-0.0014 (0.0003)
Family status			
Unmarried, no children	0	0	0
Unmarried with children	0.044 (0.031)	0.034 (0.029)	0.033 (0.029)
Married, no children	-0.019 (0.009)	-0.023 (0.009)	-0.023 (0.009)
Married with children	-0.015 (0.008)	-0.020 (0.008)	-0.021 (0.008)
Employment rate	-0.0004 (0.0001)		
Earnings		-0.0003 (0.0003)	
Net transfer			-0.0002 (0.0004)
N	2,488	2,488	2,488
Likelihood ratio	496.30	481.95	480.97

Note. Standard errors in parentheses (note that probit estimations are based on the normal distribution). Only persons 18 years and older are included. Married stands for living together irrespective of whether a couple is formally married or not.

TABLE 8.A4.

Probit estimates (marginal effects) for 1995. The dependent variable takes the value one if the individual has moved from Denmark during the time period 1996-1998. Age, gender, family status, country of origin, length of stay in Denmark, employment rate, earnings and net transfer (both earnings and net transfers measured in ten thousand Danish *kroner*) as independent variables. Non-Western immigrants

VARIABLES	(1)	(2)	(3)
Born in Denmark(second generation)	0	0	0
Immigrated >7 years	0.007 (0.010)	0.008 (0.010)	0.009 (0.010)
Immigrated 3-7	0.020 (0.010)	0.021 (0.010)	0.026 (0.010)
Immigrated <1-3	0.065 (0.013)	0.069 (0.013)	0.082 (0.015)
Female	-0.011 (0.005)	-0.010 (0.005)	-0.008 (0.005)
Age	-0.0003 (0.0002)	-0.0003 (0.0002)	-0.0002 (0.0002)
Family status			
Unmarried, no children	0	0	0
Unmarried with children	-0.011 (0.009)	-0.011 (0.009)	-0.008 (0.010)
Married, no children	-0.006 (0.006)	-0.007 (0.006)	-0.008 (0.006)
Married with children	-0.021 (0.006)	-0.021 (0.005)	-0.019 (0.005)
Employment rate	0.00004 (0.00007)		
Earnings		0.0005 (0.0003)	
Net transfer			0.0010 (0.0003)
N	4,153	4,153	4,153
Likelihood ratio	86.59	90.85	98.64

Note. Standard errors in parentheses (note that probit estimations are based on the normal distribution). Only persons 18 years and older are included. Married stands for living together irrespective of whether a couple is formally married or not.

Chapter 9
Effects on Different Parts of the Public Sector

In Chapters 5, 6, 7 and 8 we examined the transfers to and from the public sector for different groups, totally or per individual. We treated the public sector as one sector. However, the public sector consists of several parts and many decisions are made independently. There are good reasons for proceeding and trying to calculate the extent of the transfer for the different parts of the public sector. In this chapter we divide the public sector into four parts; the state sector, the municipalities, the counties and the unemployment insurance scheme.[113] Moreover, there is a part for undistributed transfers. We did calculations for 1996, a year for which we have access to a more detailed distribution of taxes, transfer payments and public consumption and investment on the different subsectors. The data that was available is constructed in such a way that the net transfers for children who are 17 years and younger are added to that of their parents.

The unemployment insurance scheme etc. is part of the state sector but we found it interesting to study separately the net transfers to the subsector that is focused on giving support to the unemployed. In addition to costs for unemployment allowances, the unemployment insurance scheme also encompasses the compensation that is given for certain, specific law-sanctioned reasons for taking time off from the labour market and for some forms of early exit, and compensation for labour market education. The revenues that go to this sector are from specific fees.

There is a specific problem when it comes to the distribution of net transfers between municipalities and counties since two municipalities – Copenhagen and Frederiksberg – do not belong to a county. These two municipalities are responsible themselves for those activities that are usually assigned to the counties (e.g. the costs for hospitals). Here the costs for these municipalities are totally assigned to the mu-

---

113 In the unemployment insurance part, the following transfer payments are included: Unemployment benefits ('arbejdsløshedsdagpenge'); leave-benefits ('orlovsydelser') for those who take leave and are being replaced by an unemployed person; two forms of early exit compensation upon leaving the labour market ('efterløn' and 'overgangsydelse'); and payments corresponding to the unemployment benefits paid to those taking part in different labour market programmes ('uddannelsesgodtgørelse', 'etableringsydelse', 'kursusdagpenge' etc.). On the tax side, two forms of fees are included ('A-kassekontingentet' and 'arbejdsmarkedsbidraget').

nicipalities, even the costs that in other parts of the country are assigned to the counties.

The undistributed part consists of some public transfer payments and some parts of the public consumption that can be distributed per individual but not per part of the public sector – we do not know which part of the public sector is responsible for the costs. The undistributed transfer payments are mainly occupational pensions for people who have been employed in different parts of the public sector. It is not possible to see which part of the public sector they have been employed in.[114] Besides that, it is doubtful whether these costs should be counted as transfer payments. In a way they are postponed wages and it would have been more correct to reckon them as costs for earlier public consumption and investment and include them in the calculations for those years. On the other hand, we should include the costs for pension obligations that were accrued during the year with the costs of the public sector of that year – but we lack the necessary information to do so. To some extent, the undistributed costs for public consumption are costs for labour market training and some public investments, for example investments in infrastructure. There is also a third part of the undistributed net transfers. Its origin is a difference between individual net transfers (micro amounts) and the total net transfers (macro amounts).

Table 9.1 shows the net transfer divided over the four subsectors. We see that there is a large positive net transfer to the state sector. This net transfer does not mean that the state has a budget surplus of the same size. Some costs for the state are not included in the calculations since they are public goods such as defence, foreign affairs etc. These costs are covered by the state. There is also a deficit in the unemployment insurance scheme that the state covers, and the state also makes transfers to the municipalities and counties some of which have not been possible to take into account in the calculations. As mentioned, there are also some costs that have not been distributed on sectors even though they are distributed on individuals. With better information, these costs would most probably have been assigned mainly to the state sector.

Table 9.1 shows that the net transfers to immigrants from non-Western countries mainly come from the municipalities. The redistribution is very large. This is even the case for the immigrants who have lived in Denmark for more than 10 years. See Table 9.2.

The information about the net transfers from the municipalities is not a measure of the municipalities' net costs. There is redistribution between the municipalities, and from the state to the municipalities depending on the municipalities' population

---

114 Ministry of Economic Affairs (1999).

TABLE 9.1.

Net transfers (in Danish *kroner*) to different parts of the public sector per person 18 years and over in 1996

GROUP	STATE	COUNTIES	MUNICI-PALITIES	UNEMPLOY-MENT INSURANCE	NOT DISTRIBUTED
Danish population (excluding those who have one immigrant parent)	30,400	100	2,700	-4,500	-10,200
Danish population (including those who have one immigrant parent)	30,500	100	2,700	-4,400	-10,200
Second generation – one Danish parent and one immigrant parent from a Western country	36,300	-1,400	2,400	-1,000	-6,600
Second generation – one Danish parent and one immigrant parent from a non-Western country	23,400	-3,600	3,000	-3,800	-6,600
Immigrants from Western countries	28,400	-300	-1,000	-5,500	-9,300
Immigrants from non-Western countries	1,800	-5,600	-34,100	-17,300	-8,400
Total	29,400	-200	1,300	-4,900	-10,100

Note: Western countries are EU countries, Norway, Switzerland, Iceland, North America, Australia and New Zealand; non-Western countries are all other countries.

composition and level of income. For the municipalities this redistribution reduces or eliminates the costs of the net transfer to the non-Western immigrants. Part of the redistribution is included in the calculations presented here but not all of it. We will return later to this form of redistribution between municipalities – and from the state to the municipalities.

There is a net transfer from the unemployment insurance scheme to all groups. It is considerably higher to the non-Western immigrants than to other groups. The amounts are larger for those who have lived in Denmark for a longer period of time than for those who have lived in the country for a shorter time (see Table 9.2). This

TABLE 9.2.

Net transfers (in Danish *kroner*) to different parts of the public sector per person 18 years and over from immigrants from non-Western countries according to length of stay in Denmark in 1996

LENGTH OF STAY*	STATE	COUNTIES	MUNICI-PALITIES	UNEMPLOY-MENT INSURANCE	NOT DISTRIBUTED
Less than one year	-19,800	-7,500	-26,900	0	-6,700
1-3 years	-25,700	-10,200	-44,400	-1,400	-8,200
3-5 years	-9,900	-6,300	-47,200	-7,600	-8,300
5-7 years	-7,500	-7,300	-46,100	-14,300	-8,500
7-10 years	800	-5,900	-45,300	-23,400	-8,300
10 years or more	18,700	-2,900	-25,800	-28,700	-9,100
Second generation	6,500	-5,400	200	-5,400	-6,700
Total	1,800	-5,400	-34,100	-17,300	-8,400

*The division according to length of stay is based on exact age. 'Less than one year' in the column for the year 1996 includes those who immigrated on 1 January 1996 or later, '1-3 years' includes those who immigrated between 1 January 1994 and 31 December 1995, etc.

can seem paradoxical since the rate of employment is higher for those who have lived in Denmark for a longer time. The explanation can be found in the fact that immigrants who have been in the country for a shorter length of time are not entitled to unemployment benefits.[115] For an unemployed person to be entitled to unemployment benefits he/she must have been employed for at least 52 weeks during the previous three years before the occasion of unemployment. While those who have lived in the country for a longer period of time pay more in fees to the unemployment insurance scheme because they earn more, the amounts they receive are even larger as they are more frequently eligible for unemployment compensation.

In the case of the counties, the net transfers are small for most groups. Nevertheless they are higher for immigrants from non-Western countries (those born in Denmark with one or two parents from non-Western countries included). When comparing individuals with different lengths of stay we find that the transfers are smaller to those who have lived in Denmark longer. The explanation is not that the costs vary, but that the taxes paid vary, which in turn depends on differences in income.

---

115 The share of those in the labour force who are insured is smaller among immigrants than among Danes. See Arbejdsministeriet (2000). The reasons for this are partly the age composition, partly differences in the degree of labour market attachment.

FIGURE 9.1.

Net transfer to the state sector in 1996 (three-year average) in thousand Danish *kroner*

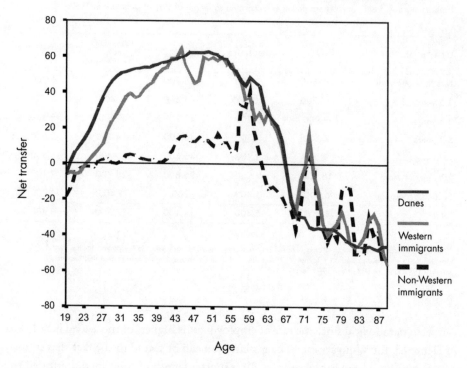

9.1 The state

We will now further examine the redistribution by age and will start with the state sector, see Figure 9.1. There is a net transfer from Danes and Western immigrants *to* the state sector until the age of retirement. The figure shows that the redistribution to the state sector is somewhat higher from Danes than from Western immigrants of active age. Contrarily, the redistribution to the state sector from non-Western immigrants is very small among those of active age. The considerably lower transfer from non-Western immigrants can be explained by the housing and social allowances that the state sector pays[116] and by differences between the groups when it comes to state taxes.

In regards to the elderly, the redistribution goes *from* the state sector to all groups. Pension payments make up a substantial part. We see that the curves for the older

---

116 The municipalities are responsible for housing and social allowances but the state shares the costs. This has been accounted for in the calculations.

FIGURE 9.2.

Net transfer to the counties in 1996 (three-year average) in thousand Danish *kroner*

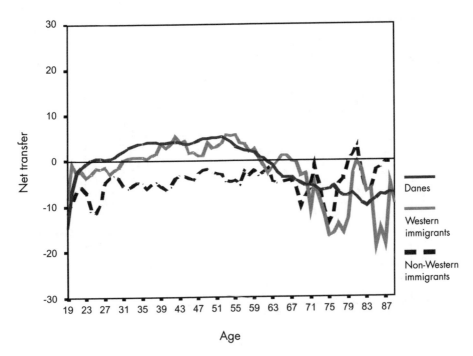

people show major variation for the two immigrant groups. The explanation is that there are few elderly people in the two groups (few in the upper active age among non-Western immigrants and even fewer over the age of retirement in both groups). Because there are few observations, this leads to the extreme values having a greater impact than they otherwise would.

9.2 The counties

Hospitals and high schools constitute the main expenditures of the counties – expenditures that are normally financed by an income tax. The pattern for the counties is easy to describe. A net transfer to the counties takes place from those Danes and Western immigrants who have reached the age where the majority enter the labour market and are below the age of retirement. To some extent there is a transfer from the counties to those who are 18 to 25/30 years of age, and considerably larger transfers to those who are over the age of retirement. This is explained by higher costs for medical care and lower tax payments. There is a net transfer from the counties to the immigrants from non-Western countries irrespective of age.

FIGURE 9.3.

Net transfer to the municipalities in 1996 (three-year average) in thousand Danish *kroner*

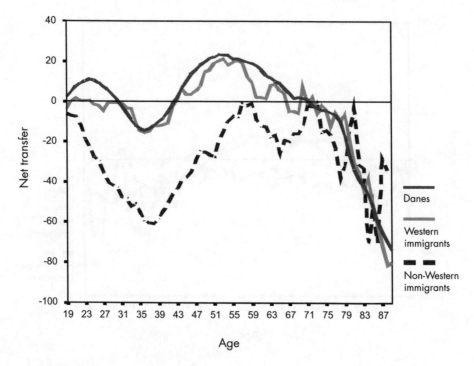

9.3 The municipalities

The next step is to examine the corresponding figure for the municipalities. We will first look at the pattern for Danes and Western immigrants. The figure indicates that the transfers *to* the municipalities take place in two age categories. The transfers to the municipalities take place until the age of 30 (the age before most people have children) and between the ages of 45 and 70 (between the time when the children start leaving home and the age when the costs for old age care start showing and tax payments are lowered because of retirement). The net transfers to those who are oldest are very high, which is due to costs for old age care.

The pattern for non-Western immigrants is the same, but irrespective of age there is a transfer *to* this immigrant group. The extent of the net transfers still varies by age in the same way as for the other two groups, but on a considerably lower level. There are several combining factors that make the net transfers from the municipalities to the non-Western immigrants very extensive. With a low employment rate and low income they pay less in municipal taxes. With many children, costs for childcare and schools become high. The low employment rate also leads to many of those who are without work receiving social and housing allowances instead of benefits from the unemployment insurance scheme.[117]

Note that there are few older people in the two immigrant groups and therefore single observations can greatly affect the pattern.

That the municipalities in the calculations here show a great deficit does not mean that municipalities with many non-Western immigrants have to take responsibility for the whole deficit or even for any part of it. There is a system for redistribution between the municipalities and also a state support system that compensates those municipalities that have many non-Western immigrant inhabitants. These systems have varied over time.[118]

Considerable changes concerning the administration and financing of the integration policy have taken place since 1999. This affects the distribution of costs between the parts of the public sector and, above all, the responsibility for various activities. Until 1999, on behalf of the state, *Dansk Flygtningehjælp* (the Danish Refugee Assistance) managed the integration of the refugees during the first 18 months after they received their residence permit. However, the municipalities were permitted to take over the responsibility under certain conditions. Since 1 January 1999, the municipalities have been responsible for immigrants and refugees who are encompassed by the law on integration (all immigrants except those from the Nordic countries, EU countries and EES countries).[119] The municipalities also took over the responsibility for teaching the Danish language to those who are not encompassed by the law on integration, but are entitled to it by the "Law of Danish language teaching".[120]

We will take a closer look at the system that has been in use since 1999. It consists of three parts: 1) A system which adjusts differences between municipalities with different tax power (45 per cent of the difference), 2) a system which adjusts for differences between municipalities with different levels of costs (where the share of non-Western immigrants is one factor in calculating the costs) and 3) a specific contribution to municipalities with the lowest tax power. Since a greater share of non-Western immigrants leads on average to a lower tax power in the municipality and to higher expenses, the redistribution system aids in lowering the municipality's costs for non-Western immigrants moving in.

---

117 See Arbejdsministeriet (2000).

118 See Indenrigsministeriet (1999).

119 See Law No. 474 of 1st July 1998 on the integration of foreigners in Denmark ('Integrationslov').

120 See Law No. 487 of 1st July 1998 on the teaching of Danish as a second language to adult foreigners; language centres, etc.

Moreover there are different kinds of national subsidies to municipalities to compensate for higher expenses as a consequence of immigrants living in the municipality. A thorough investigation of the national subsidy system can be found in a report from Indenrigsministeriet (1999).[121] First, there are specific subsidies to municipalities for the efforts they make for refugees who arrive in Denmark now. Second, there is a subsidy for refugees who arrived before 1999. Third, there is also a smaller subsidy per foreigner and year (immigrants from the Nordic countries, EU countries and North America excluded). The national contribution is calculated to be 1590 million Danish *kroner* in year 2000, 2543 million in 2002 and 3447 million in 2003.[122]

9.4 The unemployment insurance system

The fourth part of the public sector is the unemployment insurance scheme with related programmes. We have chosen to limit the figure to the 18-65 age group (with a three-year moving average it means that the lowest age is 19 and the highest 64 years). Retired individuals do not pay any fees and no compensation is given. There is a clear pattern for the Danish group; the net transfers to the unemployment insurance scheme are small for the youngest – they pay fees if they are employed but are often not entitled to compensation when they are unemployed. From 20 years of age until 35 there is a net transfer from the insurance scheme. This age group has relatively high unemployment and the unemployed usually receive compensation. From 35 to about 55 years of age the fees that are paid are larger than the compensation from the insurance scheme. The unemployment rate is rather low for this age group and the fees they pay are relatively high since their incomes are high. There is a remarkable deficit for those over 55, which reflects extensive long-term unemployment among older people but above all the fact that many of them receive early exit compensation (*efterløn*).

The age pattern of the net transfers for immigrants from Western countries is the same as for the Danes, but at a lower level. A net transfer to Western immigrants

---

121 For a critical discussion of the present system, see Lotz (2001).

122 See Indenrigsministeriet (1999). Græsted-Gilleleje municipality has made a comparison for the difference between the extra costs and subsidies according to the old rules (for those who arrived 1998 and earlier) and the new rules (those who arrived 1999 and later). The calculation is made for a family consisting of two parents aged 35-40 years, both low skilled and unemployed, and two children 3 and 10 years old. According to the calculations the new rules are less favourable for the municipality. See *Berlingske Tidende*, 11th September, 2001. We have received more detailed information from the municipality regarding the calculations.

FIGURE 9.4.

Net transfer to the unemployment insurance scheme in 1996 (three-year average) in thousand Danish *kroner*

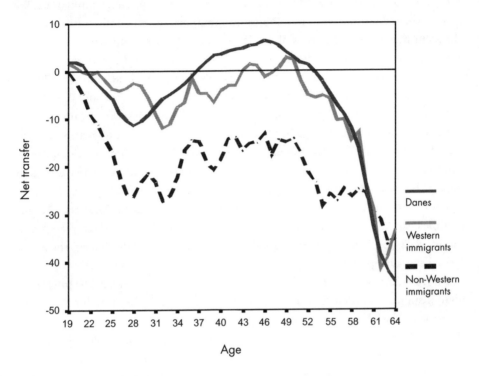

takes place in almost all age groups. We find the same kind of age variations for non-Western immigrants, but the net transfers *to* this group are considerably larger.

9.5 A regression analysis of the factors that influence the net transfers to the four sectors

In the preceding part of the chapter we have studied the differences between Danes, Western immigrants and non-Western immigrants according to age. By using regression analysis we will now study the factors that influence the net transfer to the four subsectors of the public sector in more detail. We will include the same variables as in the earlier chapters. We know from the results in those chapters that many of the differences according to age and group of origin can be ascribed to differences in the individual employment rate or earnings.

Table 9.3 shows regression estimates of the same kind as those previously shown for the whole public sector with the employment rate included among the explanatory variables. We will look at the different variables in turn. If we first look at the variables that represent different groups we see that they are rather small in most cases – the inclusion of the other variables eliminates most of the differences we saw in Figures 9.1-9.4. The exception is the coefficient for non-Western immigrants. We see that the redistribution to non-Western immigrants, given family status and employment rate, principally takes place via the municipalities. One part of the explanation may be that our classification of family status is too crude. Instead of the four categories, we have therefore tried to use a family classification scheme with 20 categories (the possible combinations of gender, married/not married, and 0, 1, 2, 3, 4-children). The absolute value of the coefficient for the non-Western group declines, but not very much, from –19.310 to –14.629.[123] An alternative explanation may be that the municipalities have special costs in connection with immigrants (Danish language courses, interpreters). In that case the costs should be higher especially during the first years of stay in Denmark. To study this, we have re-estimated the equation with the inclusion of variables for the length of stay in Denmark. We find that the coefficient is lower (in absolute value) for those who arrived ten years ago or earlier, -8.424, and consequently higher for those who arrived later (except those who arrived the same year and have only been in Denmark part of the year).

On the other hand the coefficient for non-Western immigrants in the unemployment insurance equation is positive and fairly large. One explanation for this is that Danes leave the labour market early with compensation from that sector more often than immigrants. Another explanation is that immigrants, if unemployed, fulfil less often the requirements for receiving unemployment benefits. The sign of the coefficient for female is negative for all subgroups. One part of the explanation is that women have lower wage rates so that they pay less in taxes given the employment rate. From the coefficients of the family status variables we see that the net transfer to families with children is foremost a matter of the municipalities.

We see that the employment rate affects all four sectors but that the effect is largest for the state sector, and second largest for the unemployment insurance sector. These effects are not hard to understand – the payments are larger when people are unemployed. Within the state sector, the tax payments are smaller when the employment rate is low. The state transfers also vary with the employment rate (pensions), as well as the transfers for which the municipalities are responsible but where the state sector covers a major part of the costs (social allowances, housing allowances). For the municipalities and the counties, the tax payments vary with the employment rate, and for the municipalities the payments of social allowances and housing allowances vary by the employment rate.

---

123 The corresponding change in the equation with the earnings variable is from -19.910 to -15.031.

TABLE 9.3.

Regression estimates (OLS) with net transfers to different parts of the public sector in 1996 (in thousand Danish *kroner*) as the dependent variable; and age, gender, family status, country of origin and employment rate as independent variables

VARIABLES	STATE	COUNTIES	MUNICI-PALITIES	UNEM-PLOYMENT INSURANCE (18-65)
Constant	-84.559 (1.709)	-39.710 (1.379)	72.489 (2.172)	137.753 (3.086)
Born in Denmark				
Both parents born in Denmark	0	0	0	0
One parent born in Denmark, one in a Western country	7.533 (2.384)	0.240 (0.732)	2.586 (1.153)	4.151 (0.874)
One parent born in Denmark, one in a non-Western country	7.698 (4.999)	0.410 (1.536)	2.143 (2.418)	3.647 (1.831)
Both parents born in a Western country	7.308 (5.733)	3.288 (1.761)	-0.196 (2.773)	7.975 (2.230)
Both parents born in a non-Western country	-1.127 (6.158)	1.191 (1.893)	-3.248 (2.980)	0.628 (2.263)
Born outside Denmark				
Born in a Western country	6.696 (1.728)	0.729 (0.531)	0.714 (0.836)	7.055 (0.694)
Born in a non-Western country	-3.583 (1.352)	-0.423 (0.416)	-19.310 (0.655)	10.098 (0.512)
Female	-18.425 (0.497)	-3.475 (0.153)	-7.559 (0.241)	-2.623 (0.203)
Age	3.193 (0.079)	1.956 (0.098)	-6.395 (0.154)	-14.046 (0.251)
Age^2	-0.032 (0.001)	-0.034 (0.002)	0.160 (0.003)	0.354 (0.006)
Age^3		0.0002 (0.00001)	-0.0012 (0.00002)	-0.0028 (0.00002)
Family status				
Unmarried, no children	0	0	0	0
Unmarried with children	1.656 (1.537)	-3.013 (0.478)	-78.518 (0.753)	-4.852 (0.580)
Married, no children	13.094 (0.617)	0.754 (0.190)	4.503 (0.299)	-3.224 (0.276)
Married with children	9.450 (0.706)	-2.303 (0.228)	-31.608 (0.360)	-6.170 (0.267)
Employment rate	0.875 (0.007)	0.146 (0.002)	0.343 (0.003)	0.587 (0.003)
N	138,719	138,719	138,719	113,759
R^2(adj)	0.228	0.073	0.298	0.379

Notes. Standard errors in parentheses. Individuals 18 years and older are included but for the unemployment insurance estimation only those aged 18-65 years. Married stands for living together irrespective of whether a couple is formally married or not. The employment rate varies between 0 and 100.

TABLE 9.4.

Regression estimates (OLS) with net transfers to different parts of the public sector in 1996 (in thousand Danish *kroner*) as the dependent variable; and age, gender, family status, country of origin and earnings as independent variables

VARIABLES	STATE	COUNTIES	MUNICI-PALITIES	UNEM-PLOYMENT INSURANCE (18-65)
Constant	-62.924 (1.642)	-33.888 (1.367)	87.536 (2.120)	164.325 (3.207)
Born in Denmark				
Both parents born in Denmark	0	0	0	0
One parent born in Denmark, one in a Western country	1.868 (2.294)	-0.696 (0.725)	0.373 (1.124)	0.821 (0.908)
One parent born in Denmark, one in a non-Western country	3.438 (4.811)	-0.352 (1.521)	0.379 (2.358)	-0.213 (1.904)
Both parents born in a Western country	3.478 (5.518)	2.655 (1.744)	-1.669 (2.705)	4.835 (2.318)
Both parents born in a non-Western country	-1.444 (5.927)	0.995 (1.874)	-3.689 (2.906)	-2.644 (2.353)
Born outside Denmark				
Born in a Western country	4.338 (1.662)	0.337 (0.526)	-0.139 (0.815)	3.324 (0.721)
Born in a non-Western country	-5.344 (1.290)	-0.795 (0.408)	-19.910 (0.633)	2.049 (0.527)
Female	-12.368 (0.482)	-2.509 (0.153)	-5.152 (0.237)	-1.446 (0.213)
Age	2.538 (0.076)	1.692 (0.096)	-7.136 (0.149)	-15.256 (0.261)
Age^2	-0.027 (0.001)	-0.030 (0.002)	0.171 (0.003)	0.391 (0.007)
Age^3		0.0002 (0.00002)	-0.0012 (0.00002)	0.003 (0.00002)
Family status				
Unmarried, no children	0	0	0	0
Unmarried with children	0.383 (1.479)	-3.075 (0.474)	-78.623 (0.734)	-5.285 (0.603)
Married, no children	14.762 (0.592)	1.026 (0.188)	5.090 (0.291)	-3.224 (0.236)
Married with children	7.641 (0.677)	-2.414 (0.226)	-31.943 (0.351)	-6.106 (0.300)
Earnings	0.343 (0.002)	0.056 (0.001)	0.135 (0.001)	0.164 (0.001)
N	138,719	138,719	138,719	113,759
R^2(adj)	0.285	0.091	0.332	0.329

Notes. Standard errors in parentheses. Individuals 18 years and older are included but for the unemployment insurance estimation only those aged 18-65 years. Married stands for living together irrespective of whether a couple is formally married or not.

In Table 9.4 the corresponding estimates with the earnings variable included are shown instead of that representing the individual employment rate. For three of the sectors, more of the variation is explained if the earnings variable is included instead of the employment rate. The exception is the unemployment insurance sector. This is not surprising since receiving unemployment compensation is closely (and negatively) related to employment.

The coefficients for the earnings variable are positive (and significant) and the size order is the same as for the employment rate. The coefficient is highest for the state, the unemployment insurance is number two and the municipalities number three.

The coefficients for the other variables are similar to that in the employment rate equations shown in Table 9.3. The main differences are that the absolute value of the gender effect is smaller in all four equations and that the coefficient for the non-Western group is much smaller.

The next step is to see if the effects of the employment and earnings variables differ between the groups. As in earlier chapters we have done separate estimates for the different groups – Danes, Western immigrants, and non-Western immigrants. For all three groups (and also for all independent of ethnicity) we have also done separate estimations of the equations for men and for women. In Table 9.5 the results for the coefficients for employment and earnings are shown.

In general the pattern is the same for the three ethnic groups and for men and women. There are some differences, however, which are of interest to note.

The coefficients for the employment and earnings variables in the municipality equation are higher for the non-Western group than for the other two groups. This indicates that the municipalities have much to gain by improving the employment situation for that group. On the other hand, the coefficient for the employment rate is lower for the non-Western group than for the other groups in the unemployment insurance equation. This is probably due to lower wage rates and the resultant lower fees for this group given the size of the employment rate.

To see how realistic the estimates for the various sectors are we have also made corresponding estimations for the total public sector in 1996 and the fifth sector (the part not distributed on sectors). In almost all cases the sums of the coefficients for the employment rate and the earnings of the five sectors are very close to the estimates for the total public sector. The only two significant differences are to be found in the employment rates for all women and for Danish women.

TABLE 9.5.

Estimates of effects of employment and earnings for various groups and parts of the public sector in 1996

GROUP, VARIABLE	STATE	COUNTIES	MUNICIPALITIES	UNEMPLOYMENT INSURANCE
ALL, MEN AND WOMEN				
Employment	0.877 (0.006)	0.146 (0.002)	0.363 (0.003)	0.576 (0.002)
Earnings	0.344 (0.002)	0.056 (0.001)	0.140 (0.001)	0.166 (0.001)
ALL, MEN				
Employment	0.981 (0.012)	0.164 (0.003)	0.390 (0.005)	0.564 (0.003)
Earnings	0.331 (0.003)	0.055 (0.001)	0.131 (0.001)	0.139 (0.001)
ALL, WOMEN				
Employment	0.768 (0.005)	0.121 (0.003)	0.333 (0.005)	0.580 (0.004)
Earnings	0.367 (0.002)	0.057 (0.001)	0.158 (0.002)	0.219 (0.001)
DANES, MEN AND WOMEN				
Employment	0.876 (0.007)	0.148 (0.002)	0.329 (0.003)	0.603 (0.003)
Earnings	0.341 (0.002)	0.057 (0.001)	0.131 (0.001)	0.168 (0.001)
DANES, MEN				
Employment	0.982 (0.014)	0.167 (0.003)	0.359 (0.005)	0.582 (0.004)
Earnings	0.327 (0.003)	0.055 (0.001)	0.124 (0.001)	0.137 (0.001)
DANES, WOMEN				
Employment	0.765 (0.005)	0.123 (0.003)	0.297 (0.005)	0.613 (0.004)
Earnings	0.362 (0.002)	0.057 (0.004)	0.115 (0.002)	0.227 (0.001)
WESTERN, MEN AND WOMEN				
Employment	0.824 (0.028)	0.121 (0.012)	0.392 (0.002)	0.473 (0.016)
Earnings	0.332 (0.008)	0.045 (0.004)	0.154 (0.006)	0.142 (0.005)
WESTERN, MEN				
Employment	0.891 (0.051)	0.139 (0.015)	0.452 (0.029)	0.461 (0.022)
Earnings	0.322 (0.012)	0.044 (0.007)	0.155 (0.007)	0.122 (0.006)

TABLE 9.5. continued

GROUP, VARIABLE	STATE	COUNTIES	MUNICIPALITIES	UNEMPLOYMENT INSURANCE
WESTERN, WOMEN				
Employment	0.759 (0.026)	0.096 (0.019)	0.346 (0.032)	0.483 (0.023)
Earnings	0.348 (0.009)	0.043 (0.005)	0.161 (0.012)	0.183 (0.009)
NON-WESTERN, MEN AND WOMEN				
Employment	0.857 (0.020)	0.097 (0.011)	0.569 (0.018)	0.367 (0.015)
Earnings	0.423 (0.007)	0.051 (0.003)	0.244 (0.007)	0.157 (0.006)
NON-WESTERN, MEN				
Employment	0.915 (0.025)	0.102 (0.009)	0.557 (0.019)	0.400 (0.020)
Earnings	0.377 (0.009)	0.047 (0.003)	0.220 (0.007)	0.158 (0.007)
NON-WESTERN, WOMEN				
Employment	0.779 (0.032)	0.095 (0.023)	0.581 (0.032)	0.316 (0.024)
Earnings	0.522 (0.013)	0.060 (0.011)	0.298 (0.015)	0.152 (0.011)

9.6 Conclusions

When it comes to redistribution to and from immigrants, the examination gives some clear results for different parts of the public sector in Denmark. The redistribution to non-Western immigrants takes place above all from the municipalities and from the unemployment insurance scheme. For those who have lived in the country for a shorter time the transfers by way of the unemployment insurance scheme are still small and the transfers go instead from the state sector (integration subsidies, social allowances, housing allowances).

There is considerable redistribution between the municipalities, meaning that municipalities with many immigrant inhabitants are not singly responsible for net transfers to the immigrants, but rather that these transfers are borne to a large extent by all municipalities. However, it is likely that the municipalities with the most immigrants bear a good deal of the costs themselves, especially some years after an immigrant's arrival in Denmark. This can give municipalities economic incentives to try to redirect immigrants to other municipalities. It is important to study the effects of immigration on the different subsectors of the public sector in more detail.

Chapter 10

Summary and Conclusions

Redistribution by way of the public sector is of major importance in Denmark just as in other developed countries, especially in welfare states of the same kind as Denmark. There is considerable redistribution between generations. The redistribution goes from those of active age to children (i.e. families with children) and the elderly. There is also redistribution from those of active age who are working to those of the same age who do not work.

The greater part of the redistribution takes place between Danes. The majority of the population in Denmark is Danish, and hence constitutes the greater part of both the elderly and children, as well as of the employed and the unemployed. But there is also redistribution within the group of immigrants and to and from the immigrants. It is this redistribution – the redistribution to and from immigrants – that is in focus in this book.

The immigrants are not a homogenous group. We have made a distinction between two groups: Western and non-Western immigrants. There are large differences between the two groups when it comes to redistribution via the public sector. Of course there are also great differences within the two groups of immigrants, for example between non-Western immigrants from different countries.[124] However, we will not focus on these differences here. Instead, we have consistently used the division into the two aforementioned groups.

The results show that the Western immigrant group is more similar to the Danish group than to the non-Western immigrant group with regard to the economic situation. There is redistribution from Danes and Western immigrants to non-Western immigrants by way of the public sector. The extent of the transfers from the public sector to the non-Western group is rather large.

What are the reasons for these transfers? We can point out two important factors. The first one is the age composition. Redistribution goes mainly to children (families with children) and the elderly. Few of the non-Western immigrants are of retirement age, but a great deal of them are young and many of them have children and a large part of the redistribution goes to children and families with children. If the cur-

---

124 For example, there are very large differences in unemployment between groups from different non-Western countries. See Arbejdsministeriet (2000).

rent rates and composition of immigration and return migration continue, the age composition will gradually change so that the transfers to this group will decline in the next decades. Few of the non-Western immigrants are old and the transfers in terms of pensions and costs for nursing homes are small. Gradually, a larger part of this group of immigrants will reach the age of retirement but this lies in the relatively distant future.

The second factor that affects the redistribution is the employment situation. The immigrants from non-Western countries are employed to a much lesser extent than Danes and Western immigrants. For those who have recently arrived in Denmark, this could be a temporary phenomenon caused by problems in establishing themselves in the labour market. This hypothesis is supported somewhat. Immigrants who have lived in Denmark for several years have a higher employment rate than those who have lived in Denmark a shorter time. Still, compared to Danes and Western immigrants, even those non-Western immigrants who have lived in the country for more than 12 years have a much lower employment rate. The average rate of employment will probably increase for the non-Western immigrants when the members of the group will, on average, have spent more years in Denmark. Another factor working in the same direction is that the employment rate fluctuates with the business cycle, which has had an upswing during the 1990s. A continued improvement of the economic situation can improve the immigrants' employment chances even more. There is always a risk of course that this positive trend can be broken as there are other problems for immigrants in the Danish labour market, problems that might remain even in a good economic climate.[125]

The transfers per immigrant decreased somewhat between 1995 and 1996 in real terms, but since the number of immigrants increased during the period, the total transfers also increased. Between 1996 and 1998 both the transfers per individual and the total transfers decreased. The total transfers to the immigrants decreased between 1996 and 1997 from 8,800 million to 8,000 million and was 6,400 million in 1998 (all amounts in 1997 prices). The total transfers to the immigrants measured as a share of GDP decreased from 0.81 per cent in 1996 to 0.72 percent in 1997 and 0.56 per cent in 1998. This is mainly a result of the improved labour market situation during this period of time.

Using individual data extends the analysis and gives a clearer picture of how the redistribution takes place. One conclusion is that while there is considerable redistribution *to* the non-Western immigrants, the major redistribution takes place

---

125 See, for example, Arbejdsmarkedsstyrelsen (2000) for an examination of the propensity of companies to employ different groups, immigrants among others.

between Danes. This is explained by the fact that the Danish group in numbers makes up the dominating part of the population. A large part of the redistribution is redistribution between generations, from those of active age to families with children, and the elderly. However, differences in age and family composition do not explain the major part of the redistribution to the non-Western immigrant group. Instead a great part of the net transfer is explained by the low employment rate of this group. Yet, a small but important difference compared to the Danish group is still unexplained. One part of it is explained by differences in the wage rates between the Danish and the non-Western immigrants. This is shown by including earnings – instead of the employment rate – among the explanatory variables.

It is possible to examine the effects of variations in the employment rate in different ways. One method is to see what the calculated net transfer per individual 18 years or older would be if the employment rate held a certain level. When doing so, we have combined data from 1996, 1997 and 1998 to increase the precision of the estimates. The result is that with the average employment rate for non-Western immigrants (30.6 per cent in 1998) the net transfer to the public sector becomes – 43,400 Danish *kroner* per person. By the employment rate of zero it becomes –106,200 *kroner* and by the employment rate 100 it turns out to be 98,900 *kroner*. The employment rate that makes the net transfer zero is 51.7 percent, which is lower than the actual value for the Danish group in the same year. The rate of employment needs to increase therefore by 20.1 percentage points (51.7-30.6) for the net transfer from the public sector to be zero. This means more than a doubling of the rate of employment. Another way to illustrate the importance of the employment rate is the fact that an increase in the employment rate by one percentage point increases the net of the transfer to the public sector by 2,000 *kroner* per person.

The net transfers to non-Western immigrants decreased between 1996 and 1997. This change is not explained by changes in the employment rate only. Of the decreased net transfers from the public sector to non-Western immigrants between 1996 and 1997, 1,500 *kroner* of a total of 4,000 *kroner* per person can be assigned to an increased employment rate, 500 to a change in the demographic composition (age, family, gender) and 2,000 *kroner* to other factors like changes in the redistribution system. Between 1997 and 1998 the decline is 700 *kroner*. Of this, 2,400 is explained by change in the employment rate, 200 by demographic changes and –1,900 by other changes.

When the transfers are calculated, they concern individuals over 18 years of age. Net transfers to children under 18 (schooling, childcare etc.) are assigned to the parents (the children might have been born in Denmark or in a foreign country). This means that the individual effects can concern more than one person, i.e. persons from two generations. If the calculations are changed to concern one person and one generation at a time, the transfers per person of active age decrease and the same amount is added to persons 17 years old or younger. Nevertheless, the net transfers go from the public sector to non-Western immigrants of active age and the low employment rate is crucial for this result.

The preceding analysis is used for further analysis of the total long-term net transfer due to immigration during one year. The expected total effects on net transfers to the public sector of an immigration of 10,000 Western immigrants and 10,000 non-Western immigrants are calculated. The numbers are quite large and indicate that the effects of immigration on the public sector are quite considerable. The effects on the net transfer as a result of immigration from Western countries are large and positive (from 4.7 billion to 6.7 billion depending on the discount rate used). The explanation is that the majority of the immigrants arrive at young adult age, the employment rate is high and the return migration is considerable (many leave before retirement). For the non-Western group the net transfer is large in the direction of the immigrants (from 5.9 billion to 15.4 billion depending on the discount rate used). The immigrants are, just as the Western immigrants, mainly young adults but they are employed to a much smaller extent. The fact that the amounts are large shows that it is important to make it easier in different ways for immigrants to enter the labour market.

In this study it has been possible for the first time to use panel data on net transfers to the public sector from immigrants in Denmark. The data cover 1995 and 1998. One finding shows that on the individual level there are extensive changes in net transfers to the public sector from 1995 to 1998. A part of those changes is due to young people entering the labour market and older people leaving the labour market; but there are, however, also large changes for those of active age.

Changes in the individual's employment rate and earnings are the most important factors behind changes in net transfers. This confirms and strengthens the results from the cross-section studies. If a person goes from being not employed to full employment this results in a strengthening of the public finance of an amount of 150 to 200 thousand Danish *kroner*. The marginal net transfer rate for earnings is close to 70 per cent for the total population and even higher for the non-Western immigrants.

The results show that attempts to increase the employment rate, and thereby earnings for immigrants, may have very large positive effects for the public sector. The employment rate for the non-Western immigrants has increased but it is still much lower for them than for other groups. Policies that are efficient in improving the employment situation of non-Western immigrants are therefore in great demand.

The larger part of the study deals with the total redistribution via the public sector with the population divided into subgroups. However, the public sector consists of different sub-sectors that have more or less decision-making power. In Chapter 9 a division of the public sector into four parts is made for 1996. The parts are the state sector, the municipalities, the counties and the unemployment insurance system (and other compensations). The unemployment insurance system can be seen as a part of the state sector but we have considered it to be of interest to make this division since the non-Western immigrants have a low employment rate and therefore the unemployment compensation is of great importance. The net transfers have been distributed on the different sectors. The greatest part, but not all, has been distributed.

Considering the whole population there is a considerable net transfer *to* the state sector and *from* the unemployment insurance scheme. The municipalities' and the counties' net transfer on the other hand, is close to zero. The great state surplus can be assigned to the non-distributed part, to the deficit in the unemployment insurance system (which is covered by the state sector) and to collective goods (defence, foreign affairs, etc.) that have not been distributed or cannot be distributed on individuals and where the costs are covered by the state.

Of special interest in this context are the net transfers between the immigrants (especially the non-Western immigrant group) and different parts of the public sector. A result is that the net transfers mainly go from the municipalities (34,100 *kroner* per person on average) and from the unemployment insurance system (17,300 *kroner* per person on average) and to a lesser extent from the counties (5,400 *kroner* per person) to the non-Western immigrants. A part of the explanation for these net transfers is that the immigrants pay less tax since they have lower incomes. Another explanation is that the costs for the immigrants are higher per person. First, the transfers are more extensive – higher unemployment leads to more unemployment compensation and also to more social and housing allowances to this group, which is partly offset by lower pensions however. Second, in some aspects this group is associated with higher costs since it is a young group with many students. This leads to higher costs especially for the municipalities (for childcare and schooling). The age composition also leads to higher costs for the counties for upper secondary school, and for the state sector for higher education. This is partly offset, though not completely, by lower care costs (there are few elderly people in this group).

We see that the employment rate affects all four sectors but that the effect is largest for the state sector, and second largest for the unemployment insurance sector. These effects are not hard to understand – the payments are larger when people are unemployed. Within the state sector, the tax payments are smaller when the employment rate is low. The state transfers also vary with the employment rate (pensions) as well as the transfers which the municipalities are responsible for but where the state sector is responsible for a major part of the costs (social allowances, housing allowances). For the municipalities and the counties the tax payments vary with the employment rate, and for the municipalities the payments of social allowances and housing allowances also vary by the employment rate. This shows how the net transfers to different sectors are affected by different conditions. The net transfers from the municipalities depend on the composition of the families to a great extent – a large part of the municipalities' support goes to children and families with children. The economy of all sectors is affected in a positive way by a higher employment rate. The effect is largest for the state sector and, not surprisingly, for the unemployment insurance system. Given all other characteristics, the differences in net transfers are small between the non-Western immigrants and the Danes. The exception is the net transfers from the municipalities, which are larger to non-Western immigrants. This can partly be explained by the fact that they do not have the same possibilities of receiving compensation from the unemployment insurance scheme when they do not fulfil the requirements in terms of former employment. They receive social and housing allowances instead.

It is of great importance to pay attention to the large net transfers from the municipalities to the non-Western immigrants. These deficits can affect the municipalities' propensity to receive immigrants from non-Western countries. While there is a redistribution system between municipalities, which provides for redistribution to those municipalities with low tax power and high costs, it is not certain that this is enough to cover the extra costs.

References

Ablett, John (1999). 'Generational Accounting in Australia' in Alan J. Auerbach, Laurence J. Kotlikoff & Willi Leibfritz (eds.), *Generational Accounting Around the World*. Chicago: The University of Chicago Press.

Akbari, Ather H. (1989). 'The benefits of immigrants to Canada on tax and public services'. *Canadian Public Policy*, Vol. 15, pp. 424-35.

Akbari, Ather H. (1991). 'The Public Finance Impact of Immigrant Population on Host Nations: Some Canadian Evidence'. *Social Science Quarterly*, Vol. 2, No. 2, pp. 334-46.

Arbejdsmarkedsstyrelsen (2000). *Undersøgelse af flaskehalse på det danske arbejdsmarked 1999*. Copenhagen: Arbejdsmarkedsstyrelsen.

Arbejdsministeriet (2000). *Om integration af indvandrere og flygtninge på arbejdsmarkedet*. Report from the Committee on Integration. Copenhagen: Arbejdsministeriet.

Auerbach, Alan J. & Philip Oreopoulos (1999). 'Generational Accounting and Immigration in the United States'. NBER Working Papers 7041, March.

Auerbach, Alan J. & Philip Oreopoulos (1999a). 'The Fiscal Impact of U.S. Immigration: A Generational Accounting Perspective'. Paper prepared for NBER Tax Policy and the Economy conference, November 2, 1999.

Bager, Torben & Shahamak Rezaei (eds.) (1998). *Indvandringens økonomiske konsekvenser i Skandinavien*. Esbjerg: Sydjysk Universitetsforlag.

Bauer, Thomas (1998). *Arbeitsmarkteffekte der Migration und Einwanderungspolitik: Eine Analyse für die Bundesrepublik Deutschland*. Heidelberg: Physica-Verlag.

Bauer, Thomas, Andreas Million, Ralph Rotte & Klaus F. Zimmermann (1999). 'Immigrant Labour and Workplace Safety'. IZA Discussion Paper No. 16.

Bonin, Holger (2001). 'Fiskalische Effekte der Zuwanderung nach Deutschland: Eine Generationenbilanz'. IZA Discussion Paper No. 235, June.

Bonin, Holger, Bernd Raffelhüschen & Jan Walliser (2000). 'Can Immigration Alleviate the Demographic Burden?'. *Finanzarchiv*, Vol. 57, pp. 1-21.

Borjas, George J. (1990). *Friends or Strangers. The Impact of Immigrants on the U.S. Economy*. New York: Basic Books.

Borjas, George J. (1994). 'The Economics of Immigration'. *The Journal of Economic Literature*, Vol. 32, No. 4, pp. 1667–1717.

Borjas, George J. (1998). 'The Economic Progress of Immigrants'. NBER Working Papers 6506, April.

Borjas, George J., Richard B. Freeman & Lawrence Katz (1996). 'Searching for the Effect of Immigration on the Labor Market'. *American Economic Review*. Papers and Proceedings, May, pp. 246–51.

Broomé, Per, Ann–Kathrin Bäcklund, Christer Lundh & Rolf Ohlsson (1996). *Varför sitter 'brassen' på bänken? eller Varför har invandrarna så svårt att få jobb?* Stockholm: SNS Förlag.

Butcher, Kristin F. & John Dinardo (1998). 'The Immigrant and Native-Born Wage Distribution: Evidence from United States Censuses'. NBER Working Papers 6630, July.

Butcher, Kristin F. & Anne Morrison Piehl (1997). 'Recent Immigrants: Unexpected Implications or Crime and Incarceration'. NBER Working Papers 6067, June.

Card, David (2001). 'Immigrant Inflows, Native Outflows, and the Local Labor Market Impacts of Higher Immigration'. *Journal of Labor Economics*, Vol. 19, no 1, pp. 22-64.

Card, David & John E. DiNardo (2000). 'Do immigrant inflows lead to native outflows?'. NBER Working Paper Series, 7578, March.

Chiswick, Barry R. (1978). 'The Effects of Americanization on the Earnings of Foreign-Born Men'. *Journal of Political Economy*, Vol. 86, October, pp. 897-921.

Christensen, Lars (1998). 'Immigration, arbejdsmarkedet og de offentlige finanser i Danmark' in Torben Bager & Shahamak Rezaei (eds.) (1998).

Christoffersen, Henrik & Laura Mørch Andersen (1997). *Kommunaløkonomi, flygtninge og indvandrere*. AKF rapport. Copenhagen: AKF Forlaget.

Clune, Michael P. (1998). 'The Fiscal Impacts of Immigrants: A California Case Study' in James P. Smith & Barry Edmonston (eds.) (1998).

Coleman, David & Eskil Wadensjö with contributions by Bent Jensen and Søren Pedersen (1999). *Immigration to Denmark. International and National Perspectives*. Aarhus: Aarhus University Press.

Collado, M. Dolores, Iñigo Iturbe-Ormaetye & Guadalupe Valera (2001). 'Quantifying the Impact of Immigration on the Spanish Welfare State'. Mimeo, Universidad de Alicante, November.

Dansk Arbejdsgiverforening (2001). *Arbejdsmarkedsrapport 2001*. Copenhagen: Dansk Arbejdsgiverforening.

DeVoretz, Don J. & Samuel L. Laryea (1999). 'Canadian Immigration Experience: Any Lessons for Europe'. IZA Discussion Paper No. 59.

Dex, Shirley (1992). *The costs of discriminating against migrant workers: An international review*. World Employment Programme Research. Geneva: ILO.

ECON (1996). *Innvandring og offentlig økonomi*, Report 46/96, Oslo: ECON.

Ejby Poulsen, Marius & Anita Lange (1998). *Indvandrere i Danmark*. Copenhagen: Danmarks statistik.

Ekberg, Jan (1983). *Inkomsteffekter av invandring*. Acta Wexionensia, Serie 2, Economy & Politics, Växjö.

Ekberg, Jan (1998). 'Hur påverkar invandring inkomster för infödda?' in Torben Bager & Shahamak Rezaei (eds.) (1998).

Ekberg, Jan (1999). 'Immigration and the public sector: Income effects for the native population in Sweden'. *Journal of Population Economics*, Vol. 12, No. 3, pp. 278-97.

Ekberg, Jan & Lars Andersson (1995). *Invandring, sysselsättning och ekonomiska effekter*. Ds 1995:68, Stockholm: Ministry of Finance.

Emerek, Ruth, Vibeke Jacobsen & Jeanette E. Dahl (1998). 'Indvandrere og det danske arbejdsmarked' in Torben Bager & Shahamak Rezaei (eds.) (1998).

Enchautegui, Maria E. (1997). 'Immigration and wage changes of high school dropouts'. *Monthly Labor Review*, Vol. 120, No. 10, pp. 3-9.

Epstein, Gil S. & Arye L. Hillman (2000). 'Social Harmony at the Boundaries of the Welfare State: Immigrants and Social Transfers'. IZA Discussion Paper No. 168.

Epstein, Gil S. & Tikva Lecker (2001). 'Multi-Generation Model of Immigrant Earnings: Theory and Application'. IZA Discussion Paper No. 275.

Farlie, Robert W. & Bruce D. Meyer (1997). 'Does Immigration Hurt African-American Self-Employment?'. NBER Working Papers 6265, November.

Fritzell, Johan (1998). 'Subventioner av offentliga tjänster – en fördelningsanalys av könsskillnader' in Inga Persson & Eskil Wadensjö (eds.), *Välfärdens genusansikte*. SOU 1998:3.

Garvey, Deborah L. & Thomas J. Espenshade (1998). 'Fiscal Impacts of Immigrant and Native Households: A New Jersey Case Study' in James P. Smith & Barry Edmonston (eds.) (1998).

Golder, Stefan M. (2000). 'Endowment or Discrimination? An Analysis of Immigrant-Native Earning Differentials in Switzerland'. Kiel Working Paper No. 967.

Greijer, Åsa (1995). 'Uppskattningen av övertäckningen i RTB avseende utlandsfödda med hjälp av AKU'. Metodrapport från BoR–avdelningen 1995:3, Örebro: SCB.

Greijer, Åsa (1996). 'Övertäckningen i Registret över totalbefolkningen – en studie av postreturer'. Metodrapport från BoR–avdelningen 1996:7, Örebro: SCB.

Greijer, Åsa (1997). 'Skattning av övertäckningen i folkbokföringen med hjälp av SCB:s inkomstregister'. Metodrapport från BoR–avdelningen 1997:11, Örebro: SCB.

Greijer, Åsa (1997a). 'Uppskattningen av övertäckningen i RTB avseende utlandsfödda med hjälp av AKU, 1997'. Metodrapport från BoR–avdelningen 1997:12, Örebro: SCB.

Gustafsson, Björn & Torun Österberg (2001). 'Immigrants and the public sector budget – accounting exercises for Sweden'. *Journal of Population Economics*, Vol. 14, No. 4, pp. 689-708.

Gustman, Alan L. & Thomas L. Steinmeier (1998). 'Social Security Benefits of Immigrants and U.S. Born'. NBER Working Papers 6478, March.

Hagan, John & Alberto Palloni (1998). 'Immigration and Crime in the United States' in James P. Smith & Barry Edmonston (eds.) (1998).

Hamermesh, Daniel S. (1993). *Labor Demand*. Princeton: Princeton University Press.

Hamermesh, Daniel S. (1997). 'Immigration and the Quality of Jobs'. NBER Working Papers 6195, September.

Hammarstedt, Mats (2001). *Making a living in a new country*. Växjö: Växjö University Press.

Hansen, Frederik, Sten Nicolaisen, Finn Dehlbæk & Ole Schnor (1991). *Lovmodel*, September 1991. Copenhagen: Ministry of Economic Affairs.

Hummelgaard, Hans et al. (1995). *Etniske minoriteter, integration og mobilitet*. Copenhagen: AKF Forlaget.

Husted, Leif, Helena Skyt Nielsen, Michael Rosholm & Nina Smith (2000). 'Employment and Wage Assimilation of Male First Generation Immigrants in Denmark'. Centre for Labour Market and Social Research, Working Paper 00-01.

Husted, Leif, Helena Skyt Nielsen, Michael Rosholm & Nina Smith (2000a). 'Hit Twice? Danish Evidence on the Double-Negative Effect on the Wages of Immigrant Women'. Centre for Labour Market and Social Research, Working Paper 00-06.

Indenrigsministeriet (1998). *Betænkning om kommunernes udgiftsbehov*. Redegørelse fra arbejdsgruppe under Indenrigsministeriets Finansieringsudvalg, Betænkning nr. 1361, Copenhagen: Indenrigsministeriet.

Indenrigsministeriet (1999). *Udlændinge og kommunerne – Opgaver, udgifter og finansiering*, November 1999. Copenhagen: Indenrigsministeriet.

Jensen, Bent (2001). *Foreigners in the Danish newspaper debate from the 1870s to the 1990s*. Copenhagen: Statistics Denmark.

Knudsen, Lars Kirk, Thomas Larsen & Niels Jørgen Mau Pedersen (1998). *Den offentlige sektor* (4th edition). Copenhagen: Copenhagen Business School Press.

Larsen, Knut Arild & Erik Bruce (1998). 'Virkninger av innvandring på de offentlige finanser i Norge' in Torben Bager & Shahamak Rezaei (eds.) (1998).

Lee, Ronald (2001). 'Immigration: its consequences for fiscal developments in the receiving population' in N.J. Smelzer (ed.), *International Encyclopedia of the Social and Behavioral Sciences*. Amsterdam: Elsevier.

Lee, Ronald (2001a). 'The Fiscal Impact of Population Aging'. Testimony prepared for the Senate Budget Committee, February 5, 2001.

Lee, Ronald & Timothy Miller (1997). 'The Life Time Fiscal Impacts of Immigrants and Their Descendants'. Draft of Chapter 7 for *The New Americans*, a report of the National Academy of Sciences Panel on Economic and Demographic Consequences of Immigration. National Academy Press, pp. 297-362.

Lee, Ronald & Timothy Miller (1998). 'The Current Fiscal Impact of Immigrants and Their Descendants: Beyond the Immigrant Household' in James P. Smith & Barry Edmonston (eds.) (1998).

Lee, Ronald & Timothy Miller (2000). 'Immigration, Social Security, and Broader Fiscal Impacts'. *The American Economic Review*, Papers and Proceedings, Vol. 90, No. 2, May, pp. 350-54.

Linderoth, Hans (1999). 'Offentlig sektor', in Torben M. Andersen et al., *Beskrivende Økonomi* (6th edition). Copenhagen: Jurist og Økonomforbundets Forlag.

Lotz, Jørgen (2001). 'Krise i det kommunale tilskuds- og udligningssystem?', *Samfundsøkonomen*, 2001:7, pp. 4-16.

Lundborg, Per (1997). 'Fri arbetskraftsrörlighet mellan Sverige och nya EU–länder'. Bilaga till SOU 1997:153, *Arbetskraftens fria rörlighet – trygghet och jämställdhet*, Betänkande av kommittén om EU:s utvidgning: konsekvenser av personers fria rörlighet m.m.

Lundborg, Per & Paul P. Segerstrom (1998). 'The Growth and Welfare Effects of International Mass Migration'. FIEF Working Paper No. 146, Stockholm.

MaCurdy, Thomas, Thomas Nechyba & Jay Bhattacharya (1998). 'An Economic Framework for Assessing the Fiscal Impacts of Immigration' in James P. Smith & Barry Edmonston (eds.) (1998).

Mayer, Thomas (2001). 'A frequent misuse of significance tests'. CES ifo Working Papers No. 549, August.

Mehlbye, Jill (1994). *Tosprogede børn og unge i Albertslund*. AKF rapport. Copenhagen: AKF Forlag.

Ministry of Economic Affairs (1997). *Økonomisk oversigt. December 1997*. Copenhagen: Ministry of Economic Affairs.

Ministry of Economic Affairs (1999). *Ufordelte udgifter og indtægter i "Indvandrerprojektet"*, November 8, 1999.

Ministry of Economic Affairs (2000). *The Law Model*. Copenhagen: Ministry of Economic Affairs.

Ministry of Economic Affairs (2001). *Opgørelse of nettoudgifter for 1998*, January 10, 2001.

Mørkeberg, Henrik (2000). *Indvandrernes uddannelse*. Copenhagen: Danmarks statistik.

Moscarola, Flavia Coda (2001). 'The Effects of Immigration Inflow on the Sustainability of the Italian Welfare State'. CeRP Working Paper 6/01.

Nilsson, Åke (1995). 'Brister i folkbokföringen – övertäckningen bland utomnordiska medborgare'. Metodrapport från BoR–avdelningen 1995:2. Örebro: SCB.

Österberg, Torun (2000). *Economic perspectives on Immigrants and Intergenerational Transmissions*. Ekonomiska studier utgivna av Nationalekonomiska Institutionen vid Handelshögskolan vid Göteborgs universitet.

Pedersen, Lars Haagen & Peter Trier (2000). 'Har vi råd med velfærdsstaten?'. Economic Modelling Working Papers Series 2000:4. Copenhagen: Statistics Denmark.

Rosholm, Michael, Kirk Scott & Leif Husted (2000). 'The Times They are A-Changin'. Organizational Change and Immigrant Employment Opportunities in Scandinavia'. Centre for Labour Market and Social Research, Working Paper 00-07.

Rothman, Eric S. & Thomas J. Espenshade (1992). 'Fiscal Impacts of Immigration to the United States'. *Population Index*, Vol. 58, No. 3, pp. 318-415.

Schultz-Nielsen, Marie-Louise et al. (2001). *The integration of non-Western immigrants in a Scandinavian labour market: The Danish experiment*. Copenhagen: The Rockwool Foundation Research Unit.

Simon, Julian L. (1984), 'Immigrants, Taxes, and Welfare in the United States'. *Population and Development Review*, Vol. 10, No. 1, pp. 55-69.

Skatteministeriet (2001). *Skatteordningen for forskere og nøglemedarbejdere, Skatter og afgifter – en statistik belysning*, 21.02.2001.

Smith, James P. & Barry Edmonston (eds.) (1997). *The New Americans. Economic, Demographic, and Fiscal Effects of Immigration*. Washington, D.C.: National Academy Press.

Smith, James P. & Barry Edmonston (eds.) (1998). *The Immigration Debate. Studies on the Economic, Demographic, and Fiscal Effects of Immigration*. Washington, D.C.: National Academy Press.

Statistics Denmark (1999). *Statistiska Efterretninger, Befolkning og valg 1999:5*. Copenhagen.

Statistics Denmark (2000). *Befolkningens bevægelser 1998*. Copenhagen.

Statistics Denmark. *Statistisk Årbog 2001*. Copenhagen.

Stephensen, Peter (2001). *DREAMs disaggregerade befolkningsfremskrivning til år 2100*. Mimeo, July 6. Copenhagen: Statistics Denmark.

Storesletten, Kjetil (1998). 'Nettoeffekten av invandringen på offentliga finanser – en nuvärdesberäkning för Sverige' in Torben Bager & Shahamak Rezaei (eds.) (1998).

Storesletten, Kjetil (2000). 'Sustaining Fiscal Policy through Immigration'. *Journal of Political Economy*, Vol. 108, No. 2, pp. 300-23.

Thomas, Brinley (1972). *Migration and Urban Development*. London: Methuen & Co.

Timmer, Ashley P. & Jeffrey G. Williamson (1996). 'Racism, Xenophobia or Markets? The Political Economy of Immigration Policy Prior to the Thirties'. NBER Working Papers 5867, December.

Trejo, Stephen J. (1999). 'Immigrant participation in low-wage labor markets'. Working Paper, Department of Economics, University of California, Santa Barbara.

Tseng, Yen-Fen (1997). 'Immigration Industry: Immigration Consulting Firms in the Process of Taiwanese Business Immigration'. *Asian and Pacific Migration Journal*, Vol. 6, pp. 275-94.

Viby Mogensen, Gunnar & Poul Chr. Matthiessen (eds.) (2000). *Integration i Danmark omkring årtusindskiftet*. Aarhus: Aarhus University Press.

Wadensjö, Eskil (1973). *Immigration och samhällsekonomi*. Lund: Studentlitteratur.

Wadensjö, Eskil (1999). 'Economic Effects of Immigration' in David Coleman & Eskil Wadensjö (eds.) (1999).

Wadensjö, Eskil (1999a). 'Immigration, Employment and the Public Sector in Denmark' in Kristof Tamas & Malin Hansson (eds.), *International Migration, Development & Integration*. Stockholm: Ministry for Foreign Affairs.

Wadensjö, Eskil (2000). 'Immigration, the labour market, and public finances in Denmark'. *Swedish Economic Policy Review*, Vol. 7, pp. 59-84.

Wadensjö, Eskil (2000a). 'Omfördelning via offentlig sektor: en fördjupad analys' in Gunnar Viby Mogensen & Poul Chr. Matthiessen, *Integration i Danmark omkring årtusindskiftet*. Aarhus: Aarhus University Press.

Wallberg, Eva, Magnus Medelberg & Sture Strömqvist (1996). *Samhällets stöd till barnfamiljerna i Europa*, Ds 1996:49. Stockholm: Finansdepartementet.

Wildasin, David E. (1992). 'Relaxation of Barriers to Factor Mobility and Income Distribution'. *Public Finances*, Vol. 47, pp. 216-30.

Wildasin, David E. (1998). 'Factor Mobility and Redistributive Policy: Local and International Perspectives' in Peter Birch Sørensen (ed.), *Public Finance in a Changing World*. London: MacMillan.

Wildasin, David E. (2000). 'Factor mobility and fiscal policy in the EU: policy issues and analytical approaches'. *Economic Policy*, October, No. 31.

Williamson, Jeffrey G. (1998). 'Globalization, Labor Markets and Policy Backlash in the Past'. *The Journal of Economic Perspectives*, Vol. 12, No. 4, pp. 51-72.

Winkelmann, Rainer (1999). 'Immigration: The New Zealand Experience'. IZA Discussion Paper No. 61.

The Rockwool Foundation Research Unit: Publications in English

Time and consumption, edited by Gunnar Viby Mogensen. Statistics Denmark. 1990.

Solidarity or Egoism? by Douglas A. Hibbs. Aarhus University Press. 1993.

Danes and Their Politicians, by Gunnar Viby Mogensen. Aarhus University Press. 1993.

Welfare and Work Incentives. A North European Perspective, edited by A.B. Atkinson and Gunnar Viby Mogensen. Oxford University Press. 1993.

Unemployment and Flexibility on the Danish Labour Market, by Gunnar Viby Mogensen. Statistics Denmark. 1994.

On the Measurement of a Welfare Indicator for Denmark 1970-1990, by Peter Rørmose Jensen and Elisabeth Møllgaard. Statistics Denmark. 1995.

Work Incentives in the Danish Welfare State: New Empirical Evidence, edited by Gunnar Viby Mogensen. With contributions by Søren Brodersen, Lisbeth Pedersen, Peder J. Pedersen, Søren Pedersen and Nina Smith. Aarhus University Press. 1995.

The Shadow Economy in Denmark 1994. Measurement and Results, by Gunnar Viby Mogensen, Hans Kurt Kvist, Eszter Körmendi and Søren Pedersen. Statistics Denmark. 1995.

Actual and Potential Recipients of Welfare Benefits with a Focus on Housing Benefits, 1987-1992, by Hans Hansen and Marie Louise Hultin. Statistics Denmark. 1997.

The Shadow Economy in Western Europe. Measurement and Results for Selected Countries, by Søren Pedersen. With contributions by Esben Dalgaard and Gunnar Viby Mogensen. Statistics Denmark. 1998.

Immigration to Denmark. International and National Perspectives, by David Coleman and Eskil Wadensjö. With contributions by Bent Jensen and Søren Pedersen. Aarhus University Press. 1999.

Nature as a Political Issue in the Classical Industrial Society: The environmental debate in the Danish press from the 1870s to the 1970s, by Bent Jensen. Statistics Denmark. 2000.

The integration of non-Western immigrants in a Scandinavian labour market: The Danish experience, by Marie Louise Schultz-Nielsen. With contributions by Olaf Ingerslev, Claus Larsen, Gunnar Viby Mogensen, Niels-Kenneth Nielsen, Søren Pedersen and Eskil Wadensjö. Statistics Denmark. 2001.

Foreigners in the Danish newspaper debate from the 1870s to the 1990s, by Bent Jensen. Statistics Denmark. 2001.

Immigration and the Public Sector in Denmark, by Eskil Wadensjö and Helena Orrje. Aarhus University Press. 2002.

Social security benefits in Denmark and Germany – with a focus on access conditions for refugees and immigrants. A comparative study by Hans Hansen, Helle Cwarzko Jensen, Claus Larsen and Niels-Kenneth Nielsen. Statistics Denmark. 2002.